Treasure of Pearls
Celebrating Life Lived, in Poetry

Dearest Tony & Aida

Your friendship is invaluable.
Love you all.

Enjoy reading my book.

Almeida

Selwyn Almeida

FriesenPress

Suite 300 - 990 Fort St
Victoria, BC, V8V 3K2
Canada

www.friesenpress.com

Copyright © 2021 by Selwyn Almeida
First Edition — 2021

Illustrations by Pallavi Bhatia - Mumbai

All rights reserved.

No part of this publication may be reproduced in any form, or by any means, electronic or mechanical, including photocopying, recording, or any information browsing, storage, or retrieval system, without permission in writing from FriesenPress.

ISBN
978-1-03-911432-6 (Hardcover)
978-1-03-911431-9 (Paperback)
978-1-03-911433-3 (eBook)

1. POETRY, SUBJECTS & THEMES, PLACES

Distributed to the trade by The Ingram Book Company

Table of Contents

Indian Nostalgia 1	Professions. 45
Nagoa-Verna (Goa) 3	Sacrifice 47
Goa – A Paradise 5	School. 49
Eternal City-Mumbai. 7	Decision is Yours 50
Ganpati Celebrations 8	Wake Up. 51
Fatima. 9	Bodyguards 52
Crowded Train 11	Dreaming 53
Yonge Street. 13	Hidden Talents 54
Ethnic Spaces in Toronto 14	Hunger Pangs. 55
Canadian Odyssey. 15	Life's Little Traps. 56
Condo Living. 17	You Can Lead. 57
Our Mum. 19	Grappling with Change. 58
Remembering Grandma. 20	Exercise Body and Mind. 59
Catarina's Soul's Flight. 21	Jargon. 61
Albert 23	Dad Is at Home. 63
Shivaji – The Warrior King 24	The Hobo 65
The Native Peoples 25	Lottery. 66
In-laws Can't Be Outlawed. 26	Paycheck 67
Father's Day. 27	My Bowl 69
Confusing Teens. 29	Misty. 71
Vice and Virtue 30	Autumn Colours 73
Mother Teresa. 31	Cup of Tea 74
Far from Home 33	Thrift Stores 75
Give and Receive. 35	Changing Landscape at Work . . . 76
Home Away From Home 37	Conspiracy Theories. 77
Life's Lessons. 38	Curve in Your Road 78
Good Health 39	Let's Swing Once More 79
Marriage 41	Global Humanity. 80
Our World 43	The Giant Sleeps 81
Possessions 44	Channelize Your Thinking. 82

Cool it Down 83	Proverbial Parent 106
Social Reform. 84	A Roof over Your Head 107
The Indian Thali 85	Sound Moral Judgements. 108
Happy Andy 87	True Sonship 109
The Joker 88	Solidarity Marches On 110
Divorce is Avoidable 89	Judgement 111
Relatives. 90	Angelic Values – Hope and Faith 112
Slowing Down. 91	Healthy Living. 113
The Walker 93	Inheriting Your Genes. 114
The Empty Room 94	Autoimmune Disorders. 115
Thanksgiving Day. 95	The Digestive Puzzle 116
The Evergreens 97	Mastering Work and Destiny 117
Tolerance 98	Endure the Cold Snaps 118
Love Will Calm Fear. 99	Takeovers. 119
Forty Days in Lent 100	Navigating Controls 120
Leisurely Retirement. 101	Tidy Investments 121
The Cross Never Goes Away . . . 102	Bucket List 122
Canadian Refugee Migrants. . . . 103	Long Road 123
Love is Commitment. 104	Scandal. 124
Brother's Keeper 105	Cultural Threads. 125

Indian Nostalgia

My plane lands. I know I am now home. Happy to be in the arms of Mother India
Why did I leave; couldn't I have stayed to take care of her in her advancing age?
She gave me freedom to air my thoughts and mobility to explore the peninsula
She is seen as poor in the first world, but rich in values to make you sing Halleluiah

Mother India has majestic beauty; on her head she has a tiara: the Himalayas
From her sindoor emanates the Gangotri, bringing cool water to Haridwar
Her bosom is voluptuous at the Ganges plains where the aromatic basmati grows
Her supple arms stretch from the Sundarbans in the east to Verawal in the west

Mother India is a cultural icon with a constitutional framework of secularism
Some of her myopic sons have tried to tear at the seams of her secular saree
She is resilient and beats them into hasty retreat; no wonder she is called civilized
Nations choose her to be their North Star and fashioned themselves just like her

She gave birth to Hinduism and Buddhism and has adopted Christianity and Islam
The cradle of religions has fostered peace and goodwill that the world must emulate
Her people are kind and respectful, cultured and well educated. Love blooms here
Plan to master yoga or mindfulness. Mother India will still remain near and dear

2 • *Selwyn Almeida*

Nagoa-Verna (Goa)

Nestled amidst the verdant hills of Goa is Nagoa, a quaint and picturesque hamlet
For a quarter century now, it has been home, and it has become a love blanket to me
Of all the places in this world, there is nowhere on this planet I would rather be
Its fabled beauty, with its canopy of trees, is intoxicating and mesmerizing to me

My home is not a mansion with chandeliers, and no television will you ever see
It's all wood and mud and a century old – you will think we are the old bourgeoisie
There's no radio to tell the news, no phone to air our views; it's our Isle of Capri
In this Shangri-La of ours, God is present with you and me in a loving camaraderie

Earthenware pots still don its walls, though now the home has erratic electricity
The natural spring outside enables us and the birds and the bees to live in such felicity
The morning brings lusty birds' mating cries and church bells chime as in antiquity
The stream of worshippers each day practice simple piety and harbor no bigotry

There are distractions near my home; there is a waterfall and an electronic city
At times fresh toddy, even cashew or coconut fenny, to stave you off hard reality
Large monkeys come rampaging from the hills, we have disturbed their tranquility
Luckily there is fruit on the trees for all of them; Nagoa scores high on livability.

4 • *Selwyn Almeida*

Goa – A Paradise

Goa, a tiny place in the peninsula of India, has iconic golden beaches that dot the shore
A Portuguese treasure filled with ornate churches and picturesque temples galore
A collage of cultures, where gentlemen are called patraos instead of monsieur
A westernized, engaging people, no need to play games like solitaire anymore

Traditional cuisine is fish curry rice, with shrimp and scallops, crab and mussels
Try ambo tik or cafreal, dodol or bibic if your stomach can remain unruffled
Cherussio and wild boar are discreetly available, no need to have them smuggled
If befuddled with urak, toddy or feni, sleep on the beach peaceful and untroubled

Coconut, jackfruit, and mango are nostalgic fruits, monkeys now celebrate the harvest
The men work overseas for their livelihood, leaving the rice fields unharnessed
People from all over come pouring in, which causes the locals cultural stress
Migrants value the ambience, freedom and quiet, to which they will gladly attest

Among tropical paradises, most visitors judge Goa numero uno without a doubt
You can see embalmed St. Francis, and if bad luck dogs, you can take out your Disht
The people, though westernized, organize on caste lines, and siesta won't resist
Goa stands out as a Paradise to me; to corroborate this, no lobbyist I need enlist

Eternal City-Mumbai

Mumbai is a commercial Indian hub, inhabited by convivial Kolis centuries ago
The susegad Portuguese introduced feni, siesta and port wine; sorry, no Bordeaux
The English brought language, trains and products from Manchester and Glasgow
They all established easement rights; Mumbai became a vibrant cultural rainbow

Elephanta caves, Haji Ali comfort the religious, Bollywood makes films prodigious
The stock market soars for no reason, values see-saw – neophytes, be suspicious
Palm readers at Flora Fountain peek into the future, warn of times inauspicious
If you feel cooped up, visit Alibag or Janjira, beaches to match Cannes or St. Tropez

Irani cuisine is gone, yet Bastani and Rustomji still churn out pastries delectable
Relish the pani puri, sev and ragda patties after a vigorous walk up Mazagon hill
Chowpatty Beach heralds the Queen's Necklace, lovers gaze at the Nariman landfill
The hakka cusine and kulfi are exquisite, but stay healthy and work out on a treadmill

If life goes hunky dory as it sometimes will, lay your petitions at Mahim Church
Visit the Bandra fair and eat tasty nankati, where people of all faiths converge
Start the day in Mumbia with a Kasa Kai or namaskar, wishing our neighbours well
It was home to Tilak and Jyotiba Phule, who first rang the big Indian Liberty Bell

Ganpati Celebrations

Its August, the rain's lashing eases, you hear the unrelenting beats of the dhol
Ganesha the elephant God, remover of all obstacles, has arrived, cymbals clang
The son of Shiva and Parvati, Ganesha is epitomised as lord of the multitudes
Red vermillion paste, sweet modak and laddos satiate our hunger pangs

For ten days, chants of Vedic ritual prayers made famous by the devotee Morya
The air is electrified with gaiety, the harvest is at hand, plenty to thank God for
He has an axe and a noose in his hands, has three wives: Buddhi, Riddhi and Siddhi
Devotion to him brings intellect, spiritual power and prosperity, a prospect so pretty

Freedom fighter Tilak staged yearly Ganpati celebrations at every street corner
Weaving around the laws of unlawful assembly, India united against the foreigner
To the freedoms we enjoy, Ganesha and Tilak contributed in no small measure
Come, Ganesha, come again next year, your presence brings us joy and pleasure

Mexicans venerate Our Lady of Guadalupe and have festivities like Ganesh chaturti
In times of desperation, Catholics pray to St. Jude, who rewards their perseverance
The Brahma, Siva, Vishnu pantheon resembles the Christian Father, Son, Holy Ghost
To the simple people, materially poor but spiritually rich, let's toast to their faith

Fatima

The statute of Our Lady of Fatima was finally here; we waited for this day all year
After we prayed the rosary with devotion, Dad would provide eats – sorry, no beer
The flowers were fragrant, the aroma of incense was like the oozing musk of a deer
The lamps were lit all the night, we prayed Russia would soon our Fatima revere

Three shepherd girls saw an apparition in Fatima, Our Lady's face looked serene
She warned them of calamitous events that would rattle us all, until then unseen
The two wars followed; the warnings played out like events from a time machine
Russia has come home now, it's a silver lining and historically an event Augustine

Devotion to our Lady of Fatima has diminished to a trickle in our secular state
With health care and schooling, food banks and shelters, now our minds sedate
Till our bodies bask in life's summer, we very easily all religious thoughts berate
Our Lady understands our failings, the time of our redemption does not dictate

Reverence to Our Lady is part to my faith – her love is steadfast, she never abdicates
For those who do not know her, she is at your door, just open it; it's never too late
She will fortify your lives and nourish your souls, your worries she will dissipate
I am no mystic, I don't hear voices from afar, Our Lady will all our troubles checkmate

10 • *Selwyn Almeida*

Crowded Train

The invaders came from far-off lands and left their mark on the great Indian plains
Taj the Mughals splendidly built, but the British made trains remain our cities' veins
It trundles past shanty roads and buffalo sheds, you get the unmistakable smell
Much will you learn if you listen well – things taught only at Princeton or Cornell

The stock exchange is such a foreboding place, where people risk going into debt
You can pick the dogs and stars from the chatter and safely your swift auctions set
The train is filled with mendicants begging for alms, who never issue a threat
It's such a hurried experience but amidst friends you could join in a live quintet

Now I am Toronto denizen, more stylized trains I see, seamless from door to door
Don't feel bad if they ignore you, even if you have just emerged from Seville Row
You will doubtless experience civility and may oftentimes meet your beau
What is missing is a friendly whisper or a gentle smile to make your heart aglow

There are more than a hundred different nationalities and they say it's the cause
Of this melancholy; they forget a smile or greeting causes such a profound effect
Let's abandon our fears and presumptions and let us a conversation uncork
Besides the weather, let us know how you walked, talked and held the fort at York

Yonge Street

Toronto is a vibrant, multicultural city fortunate to have a street called Yonge
It's named after Sir George Yonge, expert on antiquity, but it is an old street, not young
Voltaire called Canada a wilderness, as he did not see work commence on Yonge
Its 56 kilometers is home to people of more than a hundred nationalities, young and old

Toronto is joy in the summer, with tourists galore who shun the colder months
The weather and weatherman shut people out, yet on Yonge, all are up and about
The street is choked with bars and eateries, mendicants and fortune tellers in tow
There is always something for everyone to see, it appears such a giant road show

There is nothing unique about this city, it is not like Niagara Falls or San Francisco
You can buy maple syrup in stores, nothing more, yet memories of this city endure
People come from New Jersey and New York to stock up their pantry stores
With food and snacks and many goodies that are not available on any online store

Yonge Street has no beaches around like the lucky western Vancouver shores
It cannot hold a candle to the northern lights, which tourists flock to in droves
But it somehow fills your heart aglow and makes you come visit it for evermore
Yonge Street is a world in miniature; that's why it is now my home sweet home

Ethnic Spaces in Toronto

Canada beckons people to live here in an oasis of freedom and multiculturalism,
Cultural assimilation and integration slides into open, unabashed ethnocentrism
The Chinese visit Niagara Falls and then board buses to shop at the Pacific Mall
Indians visit Science Centre and Little India and study at Waterloo, that's the protocol

Tehran-To means Tehran in Toronto, a space to the north of Finch and Steeles
Kitchener has more Germans outside Berlin, Little Germany you cannot critique
Portuguese and Italians live on Dufferin and dine in Little Italy, a custom so unique
Punjabis live in Brampton, their colourful turbans adding to them a sense of mystique

Eglinton West is called Little Jamaica, with its jerk chicken and goat-curry houses
Chinatown lies between Dundas and Spadina, savor Peking duck and red sauces
The Russian restaurants on Steeles West serve beef stroganoff and polish sausage
Korean kimchi and Iranian polo-barberry on Finch and Yonge is common knowledge

Sociologists call this ghettoism, children call their parents' musings open racism
Your parents reminisce about their birthplace, their childhood, this is not elitism
They do not spout hatred for other races, though they practice pious nationalism
We are fellow travellers here, show tolerance even when some practice paganism

Canadian Odyssey

Majestic mountains, endless meadows, and kaleidoscopic culture make up Canada
An ocean of tranquility, kind folk that have opened to the soft drug marijuana
Maple syrup, poutine, cod tongues and beaver tails amaze even our Italian nonnas
Where astronaut families reside and dads occasionally visit to enjoy a warm sauna

The French and English migrants were the first people to colonize the reservations
Causing anxiety and turmoil to the Indigenous Peoples with a policy of assimilation
Low fertility and ageing people dimmed growth, causing new waves of migrations
Chinese, Indians, Caribbeans now altered the once-lackluster cultural equation

Passive investors derive income from capital gains and real-estate speculation
Both idle activities rewarded beyond measure with no eye on impending deflation
Don't keep your money idle, banks will help to move it to some Panamanian nation
Away from the eyes of the revenue agency who may think it's a foreign donation

While such sub-optimal economic activities in the Canadian prairies bloom
There is a baby boom, parents of mixed races, married or not, don't simply assume
Old-stock Canadians sense a cultural insecurity and disregard for old-time religion
Let's not magnify such fears; Canada is now a resilient post-nationalist nation

Treasure of Pearls

Condo Living

Condos are communal living in elevated buildings, and owners have a private space
Many folks sneer at such living and appear condescending, all with a straight face
Yet it is home to me, and as to others who have just begun society's horse race
Someday I too may tire of its virtues – hopefully when I improve my tax base

Dump the shovel and the lawn mower and begin to live a carefree condo life
It comes with security, for an extra fee, which will be valued by both man and wife
The children don't have a garden attached but will revel in the various amenities
Like library, swimming pool and exercise room, which will increase family felicity

Meeting so many kids and families each day who come from all over this world
Appreciate people you see and meet, and you may encounter a spiritual rebirth
God made us multicoloured races yet human values still endure, you will unearth
Even empty nesters enjoy bingo games where their lonely life gets a boost of mirth

Consensus in all decisions is arrived at in a monthly meeting of the condo board
You learn how not-for-profit entities work where controls are oftentimes ignored
You can live high in the sky, but don't try bungee jumping if you get bored
It is strictly against rules of sanity, though these rules are not on a bulletin board

Our Mum

Riding the elevator each Monday morning, cries one will hear and frowns one will see
Office-goers wallowing in their negativity, it doubtless affects their productivity
I remember my mum raised us seven kids and marched to work each day
A smile on her face, it appeared she held for all to see a small spiritual bouquet

She came from work each evening and would bring us the choicest treats
Her voice a sweet melody with her Que Sera Sera, which we often did repeat
Jealous Heart was my favourite, she rendered the song with such amazing grace
I have Mum's voice and winsome smile; it's a prize you can't win in any rat race

She dressed me like a king, and addressed my concerns with remarkable alacrity
Never heard her complain about the cost of living or contemplate bankruptcy
Cut her coat according to her cloth, her home remained her centre of gravity
She had many ailments but never said a word; she weathered all storms valiantly

She believed a good education was a panacea, no inheritance did we need
We strode the globe like Titans, neighbours wondered how we did succeed
Many marvelled how our self-confidence grew, being baptized with no silver spoon
The answer is our special mum; to ascribe to any another would be inopportune

Remembering Grandma

Monica was a tidy manager who needed no MBA school; her office was her home
Home skills much underappreciated are now referred to in education textbooks
She mastered the re-order point for food stocks and knew what smart goals were
Lived with my aunt and uncle with their two kids – she knew the Span of Control

Unity of command and direction, as well as a scalar chain, she directed with ease
Her varied dishes were delicious, her work stellar, she had no need to appease
Multitasking was limited to maximum two things at a time, a good mindfulness key
She loved all she did, balanced work and rest, was a sure candidate to be an honouree

Her chicken curries, mutton shakotis and fish curry and rice were such delicacies
Pastries like bibic, vorn, bhat, all coconut specialties served with aesthetic appeal
She had limited means, she put us through fire and ice to make us malleable steel
We were lucky to have in her, a great mentor; admiration for her will never cease

Monica taught us to manage by exception and she mastered the ABC analysis key
Her key result areas were family, joy and prayer; she said God would be her referee
She had no social security, she sold her gold bangles, time she could foresee
Careful asset divestments are adopted by companies planning income guarantees

Selwyn Almeida

Catarina's Soul's Flight

Catarina, your face glows, you serenely await the Angel of Death who has arrived
Your creator once breathed life into you, your soul made your living being thrive
Today his angels storm and reclaim the breath of life and will your soul archive
Till Judgement Day, when the good like you will have everlasting life, so I surmise

Some believe the soul lives forever, the body dies in a cycle of birth and death
Others believe the Angel of Death orders the soul out, the wicked sent to Hell
Some invoke the law of thermodynamics – the soul is not lost with a death knell
Others say by your accumulated karma, your soul will to some other body propel

Did these myriad details engage your attention, could you navigate its labyrinth?
Your daily tasks left you no time to consider which option was most attractive
Should you go to Heaven, Purgatory, Garden of Eden, or wander into somebody?
Religious folk grappling with issues that would disarm any student of philosophy

You lived an upright life filled with noble thoughts and deeds, evil you despised
The scales of justice will in your favour slide, the angels will to God then advise
You take your seat of immortality, a vision that for time immemorial eulogized
As you leave the earth, I may try artificial intelligence to track your soul's flight

Albert

Albert was my uncle who was more than six feet tall, he also managed an affable smile
He drove high-speed trains by day and by night practiced magic tricks just as a lifestyle
He told us stories of his railway jaunts, the wailing spirits he encountered on the tracks
We heard it all with rapt attention; his voice rang true, which made maximum impact

He was a good conversationalist, gave to all a charitable ear, thus avoiding controversy
By mastering the art of networking, you always found a friend in him and no adversary
He welcomed me into his home; at any hour, day or night, his equanimity was disarming
Being jolly was an Anglo-Indian trait; Albert embodied it even without much learning

He retired after forty years of work, his wife did likewise and their life they happily spent
By bonding thus and doing little things together they avoided loneliness and discontent
I grew up and travelled the world but never met another Albert in New York or Tashkent
Albert helped me understand that I must laugh at my foibles while in life's circus tent

The telephone rang one day, the sad news did I learn – Albert's soul left this earth
He joined the stars and the angels that stride the heavens, or possibly had a rebirth
Some people touch our lives, they say, and they cast on us such an indelible imprint
I hope people like Albert do not run out of circulation; his life was so stellar and vintage

Shivaji – The Warrior King

The steely resolve for Indian independence came through the fire and ice process
Firebrand Shivaji and Gandhi's icy noncooperation movement brought us success
The Indian people's success story in secular democracy is a model for all oppressed
His mother taught him ancient religious values, the foundation of any leadership test

The Indian countryside was then a fertile playground for invading foreign armies
Shivaji donned the mantle of bringing freedom and challenged occupation forces
From the age of 15, through daredevilry, he made deals to manage forts and horses
From 1674-1680 he was king of the great Maratha Empire, wielding power enormous

Called a mountain rat by enemies, historians compare him to Alexander the Great
With help of Maval friends, he gained familiarty with the land, useful military skills
Maintaining ties with the Mughals till 1657, in 1659 he won the Pratapgad foothills
He raided the British naval forces and had a naval presence of at least 160 ships

His path to kingship was slow as he was not a Kshatriya nor wore the holy thread
He arranged a ceremony and did atonement, convincing the Brahmin deadheads
A fearless freedom fighter, a secular leader, an avowed women's rights crusader
A patriotic Indian must epouse these values to become a democratic free trader

The Native Peoples

Native peoples in both Canada and India straddled lands from time immemorial
Possessed a rich and vibrant ancient culture unknown to people extraterritorial
Our minds deceived by tales of the native's barbarism; this tutorial fed needs revision
Their dance and craft and complex social systems made objects of our derision

Adventurers from near and far sowed fear and created easements on their land
Forced an alien governing-style religion without consulting leaders of the band
From hunters and gatherers, they got lassoed by cunning legislation backhanded
Laws made reservations and residential schools, in injustice they lived stranded

In 1982 the wrong was recognized to prevent assimilation being termed genocide
Meagre doles cannot undo the harm done, needed now is Truth and Reconciliation
True autonomy and relevant education, good jobs and respect, to avoid ruination
First Nations, Metis and Inuit, we beg forgiveness, realize we are still on probation

The bright light comes from schools now, where all are taught genuine equality
Examining our historical wrongs through introspections makes for a wise polity
We need to digest the thought that there is no life which is high quality or low quality
The 461 tribes in India and 3 Native peoples in Canada will then live in tranquility

In-laws Can't Be Outlawed

Genesis 2:24 says God created man and with man's spare rib came woman
It exhorted that a man would leave father and mother and cling to his wife
For adultery, Moses permitted a man to divorce his wife and take another
Moses commanded that people should also honour their father and mother

Spouses conveniently quote the cling argument and neglect the honour one
Cherry-picked Biblical paras create conflicts and cause parents dishonour
Ecstasy with arrival, a spouse cannot extinguish our parents' medal of honour
They deserve our care, caring spouses understand, don't ever be cornered

Marriage is not doing your spouse a favour; in-laws come into your sphere
They are now woven into your marriage fabric, do not ties with them sever
Your spouse has parents who they love and revere, learn then to persevere
Keeping the commandment will bring God's kingdom, such joy it engineers

Loving and caring for both parents and in-laws is a special skill of diplomacy
Embracing it, you win friends, keep away enemies, settle disputes amicably
A jolly spouse gladdens the children, joy is infectious, and it works magically
Italians will attest that caring for in-laws combines both sense and sensibility

Father's Day

Mothers have been deified through the ages; fathers expected to earn the wages
Father's Day is a breath of fresh air, 'thanks, Dad' cards come in with catchy phrases
You are not an anchor or a sail but a guiding light when darkness or storms rage
Once you left at dawn and got back at dusk, now Dad's roles from the dark ages

Your affection and family involvement promote the kid's emotional development
You will become a sensitive, naturing caregiver, spread love inside your tenement
If you are a pillar of strength and discipline, it helps foster character and affection
Your daughter's confidence, poise and self-esteem grows in geometric progression

A rich dad is one whose children flock to him even when his hands are bare and empty
Some wish for their dad's inheritance, such sentiment can make any dad feel testy
You are expected to not only sire kids but have the courage to raise them zestily
Add some humor and honesty, unconditional love increases bonding chemistry

If you feel Father's Day is so much hype or just a marketing ploy, you may be right
Endless commerce needs to empty its inventory shelves and make them light
Enjoy the attention and gaze and to all who compliment you, try to remain polite
Time to take stock of your not-for-profit goals while enjoying the dazzling spotlight

Confusing Teens

The teenage years sometimes bring tears of joy and grief into your parents' eyes
They find it hard to believe that their kids have grown so fast, much to their surprise
The rolling years edge on, and with them, much confusion springs at times in a disguise
The days of singing lullabies fade away when suddenly hormones like a geyser rise

Every attractive person among your peers suddenly becomes the cynosure of your eye
An attractive sports car becomes the car to covet even if you are not the King of Brunei
The palatial house you see becomes a dream home even if you are financially bone dry
You hero-worship people who are men of straw in spite of them wearing a black eye

Should such thoughts take hold of you, learn to separate the wheat from the chaff
Lust and possessiveness are drives that may lead to gaffes; don't mix with the riff raff
A car is expensive to buy and maintain, question if you need it; a car is no golden calf
Your home can be small where joy abounds, and worry drowned in a good belly laugh

Honour your parents who have sacrificed so much, missed a night out to be with you
The teachers who spotted your talent and encouraged you with their unique world view
Be grateful to friend's patience with you even if they did not share your point of view
Cool down your raging desires and to evil thoughts learn to say a loud No Thank You

Vice and Virtue

The teenage years heralds' seismic changes silently in you both in head and heart
Parents, teachers, siblings and friends play their part to give your life a head start
Loving and caring, joyous and sharing weaves your character making it state of art
Fashion your life with virtues galore and quickly fill your characters shopping cart

You may still not be a Venus or an Adonis you planned on being, yet never forget
To stave of **wrath**, the intense anger burns down life's barn, all good it offsets
Be wary of **greed**, the wish to possess, its treacherous bait may bite like a bullet
Don't practice **sloth**, rendering you inactive, stay chirpy like a merry cricket

Shun **pride** or inordinate self esteem; stay humble because pride has a fall
If **lust** or excessive sexual desire troubles your soul have a cold bath by nightfall
Envy bugs do bite, then wish well the success of friends, dame luck will cycle in
Gluttony or eating in excess reminds us that Gluttony can never be a secret sin

If luck eludes you, and ill health attends you remember avoiding the 7 deadly **sins**
Character is a sum of good and bad habits cultivated since our earthly life begins
The fear of the Lord is the beginning of wisdom, keep him as your good Shepherd
And by your Love men will know God loves unfettered lives and on you joy bestow

Mother Teresa

At age twelve, Teresa dreamed of a religious life, at eighteen it became reality
In a familiar world of child prodigies, she dared to usher in a rare spirituality
Cared lovingly for the hungry, naked, homeless, blind, with unseen vitality
People uncared for who were forgotten, felt love had finally dispelled fatality

Dreams need blueprints and tidy budgeting. Teresa begged for food and supplies
She experienced doubt, was spat on by some and for her entreaties was chastised
Comforts of convent life were on her mind but on hard work she never compromised
Charity begins when it hurts, convictions that got this noble activity motorized

The Bengal famine of 1943, a natural catastrophe, brought much death and disease
Teresa had a call within a call, she adopted the poverty of the cross, her magic key
Started the Missionaries of Charity, a paradigm of love that grew large as a fig tree
Naysayers parodied her work, but she bore those indignities with Christlike serenity

Lepers and HIV victims found comfort in her, the kingdom of God had just arrived
Its pristine values of charity and love erased stigma and fear that dogged mankind
Religion or nature of ailment were not discussed, out of respect for all humankind
Teresa showed us the way, let no person in need of love be ever quarantined

32 • *Selwyn Almeida*

Far from Home

I heard it said that east is east and west is west, and the twain shall never meet
To test it out, I travelled west 8000 miles but somehow retained my eastern soul
Our diet was simple meals, the love of parents, caring for the young and the old
Life was simple, and we always asked God to keep us in his protective fold

I am now grown and come of age and in need of marrying a friend who is true
Wonder if I will ever find a soulmate that, like my dad, has youthful mirth too
I will pray ceaselessly and storm heaven's door because much is promised to His people
Seas once opened at His command; He will undoubtedly find a mate for me too

But before that, I find it hard to know; I may have to date a dozen men or more
It's so quaint that I could become a commodity, with such permissiveness galore
My soul rebels, my head aches at this, I wish not to trot like this anymore
We miss the point that God's co-creators we are, He planned so much for us

Marriages are made in heaven they say, but consummated on this earthen floor
Yet we doggedly seek depravity by laying waste our powers on mindless ecstasy
If we should raise men of steel and gals of grit, we will have to reckon the cost
And to nourish our souls and make them robust, we need to emulate the eastern soul

Selwyn Almeida

Give and Receive

Success is a goal most people hope and dream for, a fancy house and car in tow
Vacations, happy kids, and wife content, much money in the bank to store
Goals exceeded, worries behind, life's vicissitudes could harm them no more
Such happy bliss conjured by modern folk, factors not in happiness anymore

The common folk who such benchmarks fail to cross do not such thoughts behold
Their lives are filled with worry, paying bills, and replenishing their pantry store
They realize that turbulent times means reducing their concentric wants
To bond, love and pray to God to give them their daily needs and not their wants

The happiest are ones that just get by each day; success is a hopeless dream
With this knowledge of wisdom, we found we must resolve each day
To empty our closets, hearts and vaults to all our unfortunate friends
It's in giving that we receive. Love, if not success, true happiness portends

The dam releases water and Mum suckles her child, both their integrity uphold
It is in ceding our soul that we reap a harvest of diverse treasures untold
Don't wait for donation receipts to offset your tax, open wide your hearts
Success will enter your lives and stay; all your sorrows will very soon depart

36 • *Selwyn Almeida*

Home Away From Home

Home is a comfort zone, each person and thing you love in their appointed place
If you leave home for study, travel or work, you may encounter an obstacle race
Should this make you poker-faced, relax, your mind will grow at a geometric pace
This was the story of the master race who sailed the seas and won their sack race

Human values are not the preserve of only the noble kind; they reside in each of us
Small cultural differences you will learn; respect them in life's little school bus
New friendships will you forge which may leave on your life an indelible imprint
The world is made of more than just the family of whose love you wax so eloquently

Sojourn to the Arab world made me realize how they valued decency and family
Caring for the young and old and providing amnesty to those in need
You can avoid bankruptcy by borrowing loans that are interest free
Beverages are served with civility; sip it, lest it be construed as impropriety

Wanderlust took me to Canada, a land where cultural groups respect diversity
Not willingly but with rules carefully written into their code to extract conformity
The individual is supreme, and people believe in other centredness and charity
Landscape is so majestic – that you will see if you row away from the home like me

Life's Lessons

Kids get lavished with love from both Mum and Dad, and grandparents
But when it comes to teaching kids, all agree it's not a game for just the two
Teachers, friends and acquaintances, and people riding the elevator too
But after all, consider what matters most is what Dad and Mum teach you

Your sparkling smile, your polite and winsome ways, you pick them at your home
From Dad and Mum and siblings whose love for you lives for evermore
Good nature and tidy manners are seldom learned in libraries or in a book store
You a miniature of your parents will be, so cherish the good and the bad ignore

Dads and Mums, be good custodians to the children that you chance to raise
They will be then be your ambassadors and will render you thanks and praise
When others notice their geniality and their manners abundant store
They will know you were selfless and your honesty in your actions showed

We have a dad and mum for a reason; that was God's wonderful loving plan
We hope they keep their sacrament tied always in the invisible tread of Love
Their joys and small sacrifices are for us to see, it is only through their example
Will they life's lessons teach. And so, I will always want both Dad and Mum for me

Good Health

Your person combines the body, mind and soul, each element needs balancing
None greater than the other, ignore any of these three and life will be agonizing
Life is long and winding, and staying whole in mind and body keeps the soul robust
Keeping your health vigorous is akin to managing your life's savings bank trust

Good health is not only the absence of some infirmity; it is an index of your sanity
Relish what you eat, don't eat for two when you are all alone, that is gluttony
Rest and sleep at regular intervals; it invigorates and in you brings harmony
When the day is done, be contrite and pray; God is our father, not just a fantasy

Till the age of forty, which is life's summer, no doctor or a priest would you need
Thereafter, your body parts will need repair – panic not, nature reduces our speed
Be aware and inspire all who live with you, and to their good health pay heed
The family bus will trundle through life merrily; it's a testament of your sagacity

Good health has many enemies in bad habits: drinking, smoking and overeating
Keep a watchful eye on these; fleeting pleasures they bring, yet are self-defeating
By chance if you do not have lucky genes and don't live four score years or more
By tending to your body, mind and soul you will enjoy true happiness galore

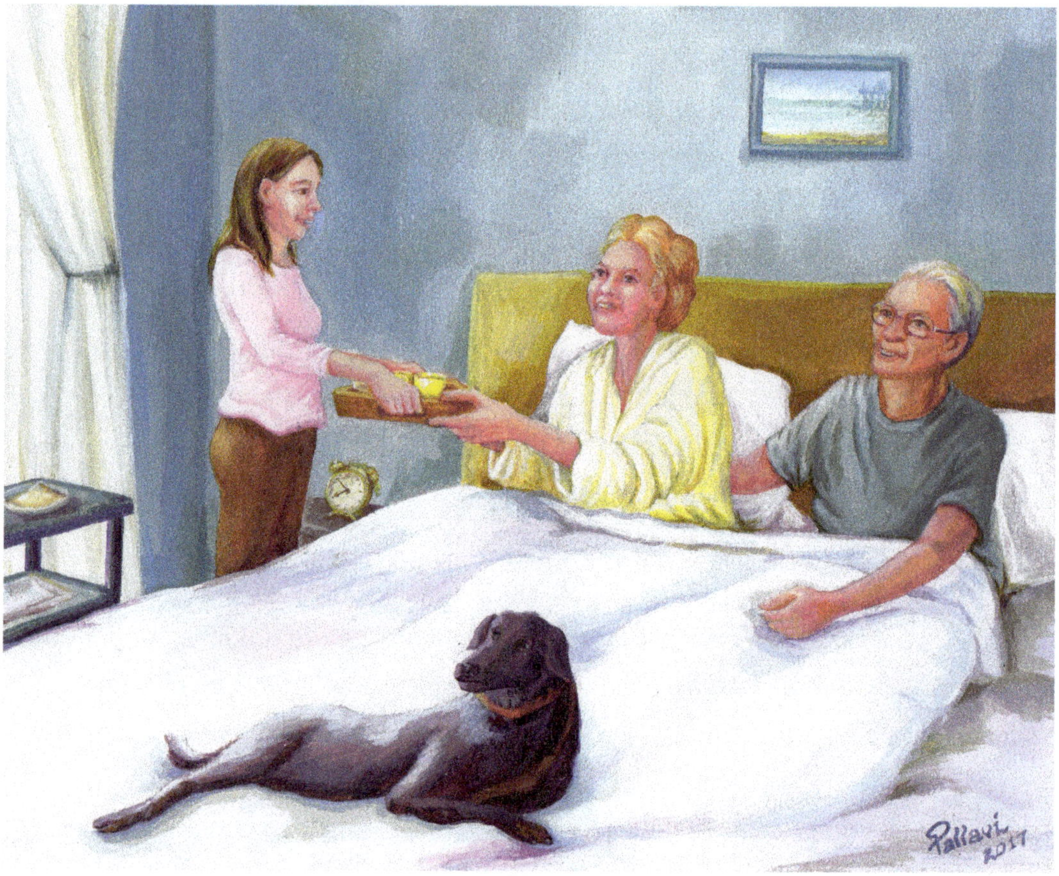
Pallavi
2017

Marriage

The carefree teenage years pass swiftly, we are now required to stand on our feet
Take up a trade, get a job, buy a home and move out and join the main street
This transition turns into a pressure dome till we find a spouse true and sweet
The search ends with a contract of marriage, no more can you do a trick or treat

Some call it a social contract with possibility of a divorce, an escape for a price
Some call it a sacrament made before God that must be maintained till one dies
It gets you a mate and possibly hot meals subject to availability of pantry supplies
A steady job is like a ballast to marriage, its value more than one will ever surmise

Children are a consequence of marriage, God's gift to man since the world began
You inherit genes of your ancestors and are not part of your parent's master plan
It is hard work thereafter, just like rigorous imprisonment for possibly seven years
Repay them with gratitude, both in cash and kind, love may bridge the arrears gap

Our parents are God's co-creators, their love is tested and at times they succumb
This brings them privations and breaks the home, making us look like bubblegum
The books want you to choose a mate who is patient and kind, faithful and true
Wish we could have such world view or call on God to help with a judicial review

Selwyn Almeida

Our World

Earth is our mother and the Sun our father, the moon and stars providing company
They such a bonding fraternity make; we wonder if they practice matriarchy
Mother is gentle and nourishes us all, Father always seeking to keep us warm
The moon dazzles lovers, the stars the zodiac make, all to symmetry conform

The Good Lord made us such a happy extended family that worship him we must
For he made us custodians of the universe and on all our shoulders thrust
The worthy task of securing this family for posterity, in a task we must be just
If this gentle bond we break with our insanity, we will violate an inviolable trust

While some discuss who this family made, let's not indulge in sterile thought
But retain Mum's vitality through her renewal before to us much pain is fraught
And keep Dad's sanity by avoiding a nuclear bash, of which, will our nemesis bring
The stars and moon the heavens will guide, let's know this is no ordinary thing

We must ignore the cry of those who scoff and think it's one grand conspiracy
Of armchair pundits or laisse faire economists or some sort of liberal tyranny
To help keep our universe strong and free and live a million years and more
We will have to work with abounding zeal and maintain abundant espirit de corps

Possessions

My credit card is a comforting presence; it makes my journey smooth and carefree
I don't carry guns or body armour, as I luckily have no enemies lurking in trees
I acquire varied things I never use; I think I must now gift them to the diocese
My home is a virtual storeroom; hoarding does not slow even if my wages freeze

A thief entered my home one day and decamped with my gold and electronics
I found my private space violated, you would laugh and sneer at my histrionics
To add insult to injury, my trusted banker embezzled my hard-earned savings
All because he thought I would never ever know, thus supplementing his earnings

The road of Life is long and winding, much will you acquire and sometimes lose
When people lose things it gets others amused; when we lose, we get the blues
Filled with abject despondency, instead of grieving, view the TV's world news
It tells us of destructive storms and bombings, providing our loss with an overview

Vacations, costly cars, homes and bulging bank balance makes life appear serene
This stupor could be rattled if our possessions are lost or evaporate like benzene
Acquire a good education, arm yourself with human values that are Augustin
Moderation, gratitude, generosity, good health will keep you always evergreen

Professions

A doctor studies how to cure the sick, yet we say 'physician cure thyself'
A teacher studies to teach us, yet we know only the Spirit can guide us
A priest studies to teach us spirituality, yet he must first understand philosophy
A cobbler learns to mend our shoes, yet cannot help us to mend our conscience

A carpenter knows to repair wooden objects, yet he cannot repair a wooden heart
An artist does creative work, yet fails to realize he must be out of step with his time
An engineer makes practical solutions, yet a third of them could fail in basic math
A fireman extinguishes flames, yet can't put out a fire in his own rabbit hole

A nurse learns to care for the sick, yet to get a good nurse you must be patient
An electrician fixes lights, yet cannot understand a blinking pacemaker
A plumber learns to repair pipes, yet he gets the blues on Mondays and won't tell you so
A tailor knows to work with cloth yet finds it hard to cut his coat according to his cloth

A chemist knows to dispense drugs, yet goes blank when asked what sexual chemistry is
A sailor works on a ship; he joined it to see the world but all he saw was the sea
Youth is a period before maturity when they find it hard to get out off their life's web
God created the universe, but He wants us to remember to do all what we do, and do well

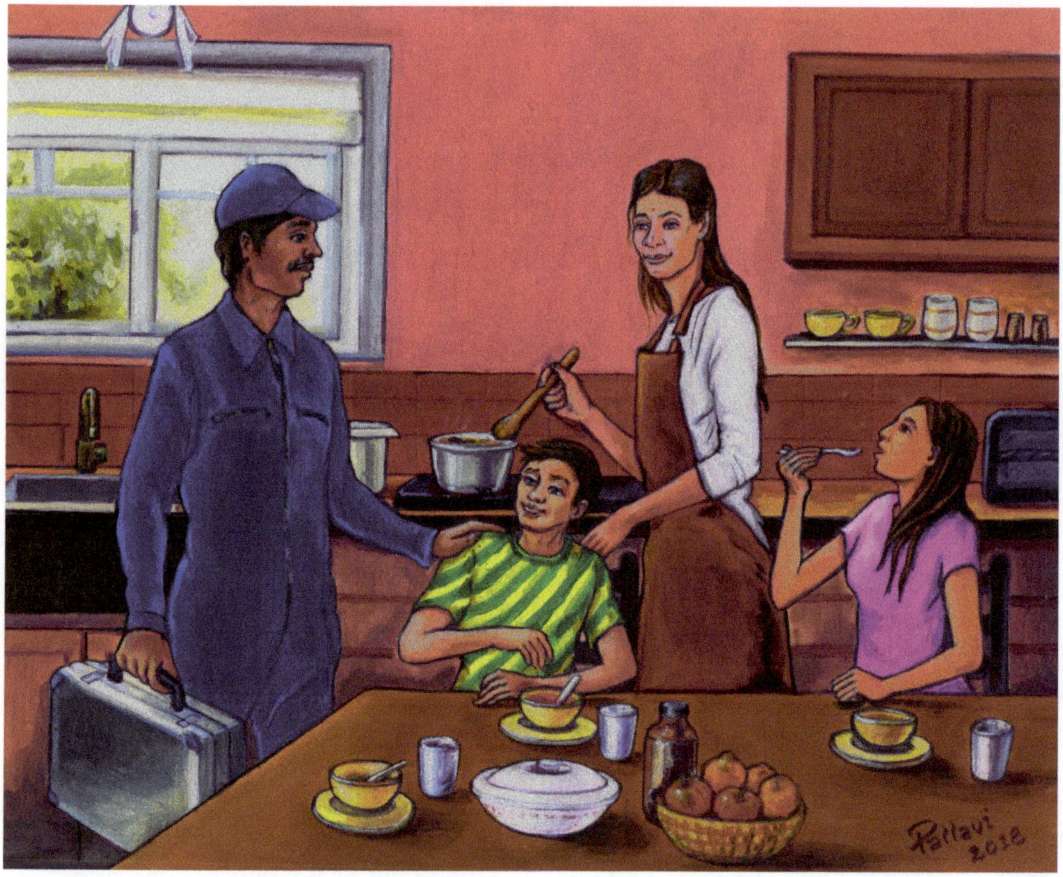
Pallavi
2018

Sacrifice

When perchance the wind at your back rides and your face shines like a superstar
We tend to ascribe it to Dumb luck, a lucky charm or alignment of our stars
Seldom do we ascribe it to our dad and mum who played life's game of parallel bars
And nurtured us from childhood and even fashioned us to be like Venus or Mars

They stood like a rock between us and the cold, seeing that on us no injury befalls
Their meals were remainders after the food did their rounds with us at nightfall
They were industrious beyond measure and burned their life's candle at both ends
Sacrificed their life to give us a chance to succeed, which we must commend

When faced with hurdles, let's never blame our parents, who gave us so much
Or paint them as vainglorious villains who caused on us misfortune to befall
We must to ourselves be true and reorder our lives, in it some character install
Mum and Dad must be emblazoned in our hearts and on our mantle stand tall

When Dad and Mum grow old and are feeble with age, let us their watchful eye be
While we cannot overturn their oncoming senility, let's avoid for them the ignominy
Of loneliness and to them good friends be, treating them with respect and dignity
Their sacrifice then will not be in vain and our lives will overflow with tranquility

Treasure of Pearls

48 • *Selwyn Almeida*

School

Saint Mary's was a Jesuit school to which in my childhood I reluctantly went
Vows of poverty, celibacy and obedience much did the Jesuit's soul torment
These extreme vows made their lives discontent, which also made all of us resent
Inspite being good educators, their strict discipline would be a reason to lament

To set the scales of justice, to them we must be fair, they made us the men we are
Taught us to obey the commandments and ensure our character we do not mar
In our lives they wanted us to keep five principles and maintain them as bell jars
And not to chase a girl, or touch their bodies, even if they were blazing stars

School friends of mine get nostalgic when they talk of those halcyon days
And wish the clock stood still, hoping that their fantasy lifts their life's current haze
Each precious moment unfolds treasures new, so I don't dwell on those early days
The past is a stale cheque, they say, today is ready cash; keep away from the maze

I to five principles was true, just as the Jesuits said and lived till now an integral life
Comfortable with my good and bad as well as my mediocrity, that's my way of life
Keep in mind the commandments ten, and to the five stages of life be true
You will soon image the famed Jesuits who taught life's baby steps at school

Decision is Yours

School was fun, the rain, slush, friends, but dreaded was the homework we were laden
Farming was great, the corn, cows, had to see there was work for all the maidens
Teen age was cool, skills to learn and decide what would make a good life trade-in
Decisions we had to make including whether to learn tech, Spanish or Mandarin

Learn to manage a crisis, focus on plans, avoid procrastination and reduce stress
Watson with low IQ invented DNA, Steve Jobs the techie lived at no fancy address
Franklin Roosevelt, paralyzed waist down by polio, did not his personality depress
Gandhi and Mandela against all odds worked to help people who were oppressed

Simple folk can live extraordinary lives; decisions help transform you from within
Examine choices and mentally resolve to do, delegate or eliminate mental tailspin
Master how to separate the dogs, cash cows and stars, an investor's basic lynchpin
Stocks and currency, buy low, sell high; don't need to go to Harvard or Princeton

Good decisions may sometimes lead to poor results; you can still say you tried
Marriage is luck, where the best of men at times do not find a compatible bride
Raising a family is difficult at best, endure pain you must keep at times classified
When in doubt, ask the Lord for help; he is the Living water, he is not yet calcified

Wake Up

A twelve-year-old carpenter's son learns the pedagogy of preaching at the temple
He stands up for the forgotten and oppressed and then is construed as a rebel
Crucified for preaching equality and love of neighbour precedes love of the shekel
He did not accept social injustice; his actions reminded the sick they were special

Six centuries later a forty-year-old orphan hears the revelation of Angel Gabriel
He woke up and preached that God is One and surrender is a test of the faithful
Through constant faith and prayer, charity and fasting, we show we are grateful
When all have a place at the table, we celebrate that we made society more stable

Through the ages holy men came to wake us from our lazy self-preoccupations
Reminding us to rise and reach to all who are victims of social discrimination
The Good Lord made all of us for a reason, no one should suffer abandonment
Let's stop pious pontificating and wake up, we are all sons of God's great nation

Wake up and vote at the polls, we make our society, let's not blame politicians
Let's care for the homeless and provide all healthcare, on these take positions
The blame game is easy but inexcusable, on common matters let's build coalitions
Just like skiers who wake up and stay alert about changing weather conditions

Bodyguards

A secure home, a supportive family and friends makes us look like a lion in a den
My bodyguards are three: white blood cells, T cells and antibodies, all wise men
A formidable group, part of my immune system, but they succumb now and then
To the onslaught of bacteria, viruses, fungi and parasites like a wolf in a sheep pen

My bone marrow, spleen, liver and skin are reasons why my bodyguards exist
I feed them nutritious food each day, stay clean and safe, on these they subsist
When hordes of bacteria or virus attacks, my immune system goes into curfew mode
Surrounding these invaders military style, my health temporarily at a crossroads

The infectious agents come through our skin, contaminated food, air and ticks
Our bodyguards at times fold, the enemies spread around cells like a row of bricks
And give out chemicals called toxins, which damage tissues, keeping us transfixed
The West Nile and Zika virus have moved north, it seems like a health eclipse

Some lucky folk live a long and healthy life, sure they have resilient bodyguards
Probiotic bacteria keep our bodies in balance, so make right your health scorecard
The ecosystem depends on the labour of good bacteria aiding the nitrogen cycle
Bodyguards, please consider bacterial nobility before executing the next reprisal

Dreaming

I have reached the rapid-eye movement or the fifth stage of sleep, its deep sleep
My mind enters uncharted territory, entertainment, disturbance, bizarre creep
I am on a reckless ride, conjuring images and stories, cannot figure how to beep
Wish all this had a purpose or provided me a premonition of the taxman's sweep

Experts say we dream four to six times a night, but I daydream often when bored
Gaining the prized medal, or solving an odd puzzle or slicing demons with a sword
Is there a part of me, I don't know, or is it my id, ego or superego I long ignored?
Dreams solve problems, processes emotions, straightens my life's drawing board

If you get dreams, don't be alarmed; avoid drugs and alcohol, surely they harm
And contribute to negative emotional content, strange dreams you cannot disarm
Women dream of family, men cavort with women, captives on their prison farm
Dreams reflect our subconscious desires – don't wake up and purchase a firearm

You may dream of solving the world's poverty, or how to restore nuclear sanity
Or wipe the tear of an orphan. Let's then band together to eliminate inhumanity
The three wise men saw a star in a dream, which led them to the child in agony
Let's come together, be our brother's keeper, and rid this world of its maladies

Hidden Talents

Positive corporate culture recruits, develops and retains the best talent it owns
It fosters creativity and passion and ensures its rightful place on the Dow Jones
Ignoring talent is a waste of resources, an ominous sign to ready the tombstone
Managers who fear talent will drag the company down a hole all so well known

All are born unique, with varied gifts to serve one another, God's kingdom is here
Value the gifts you have, use them in proportion to your faith, and to all endear
Whitney and Lata, both melody queens, started praising God early in their career
Shakespeare and the Psalms, literary and spiritual gems, now readings to revere

During prayer ask that your life's purpose be revealed and your talents be seen
Multiply your talents; it gladdens you even when they are not well received
You may have gifts of healing, helping or administering – put them in other's service
God blesses the humble; in loving your neighbour, you will encounter life's purpose

Talent management is a business strategy; it makes for sound succession planning
To stay on course, companies are investing in stellar folk with talents outstanding
Fear not emerging talent; reward their services, it's good business understanding
See talents in others; it will ensure your deeds of karma remain in good standing

Hunger Pangs

The tall Maratha men loading wheat in a truck sit down for their midday meal
Dry wheat rotis are relished with pickled chilies and onion, no meat or cornmeal
Strong men of Upper Egypt have a khubz or wheat bread with falafel and herbs
Hardworking Chinese labour sit down with a bowl of tasty noodles and vegetables

Simple people leading ordinary, healthy lives and passing hard days in quiet piety
No roast beef well done, no caviar, no shark fins all reserved for the well heeled
Ask a child their choice meal, chicken and hamburger dishes are usually revealed
Parents, society and fast food have played a hand in creating a hunger battlefield

The elusive rain at times plays truant, causing untold hardship and bitter poverty
Sustainable agriculture and harnessing renewable resources must be our priority
Reduce meat and fish to a quarter of our meal plate, let's have balanced diet clarity
Our colons find protein food indigestible, be mindful of this and restore sanity

Let's call in a stranger and give them a meal, or fill the coffers of any true charity
We on this earth are bound together, let's banish hunger and eliminate disparity
The holy book tells us of poor hungry Lazarus picking scraps. Dives had no mercy
Let's not wait for Judgement Day, it may be late to get water though we grow thirsty

Treasure of Pearls • 55

Life's Little Traps

The journey of life can be joyous if you can avoid a minefield of unexpected traps
Examine, judge and test a product on buying; it's called 'buyer beware,' a legal gap
In contracts, exit is possible for a mistake of fact, mistake of law can cause mishap
You own what you find, possession is 9/10ths of the law till the true owner arrives

If you take an animal on lease, the lessor owns the calf born in the period of lease
A prenuptial contract keeps assets of couples separated you can now live in peace
Employees sign a confidentiality clause as it deters theft, and keeps away the police
Free speech is in the constitution enshrined, hate speech spoils community peace

Using borrowed money with a credit card is leverage that cannot be sustained
Sudden expenses come, your income must underestimate, expenses constrain
Luxuries are not affordable at times, enjoy little things, don't appear to be vain
Teach kids about pitfalls of substance abuse, stay away from cocaine and codeine

Stay informed of possible elder abuse when your parents grow old and need help
Clean clothing and safety will keep your parents free of deadly viruses like strep
The aged suffer possible financial, physical and emotional abuse, stay prepped
Be alert even if you have benefits from cradle to grave, life's little traps intercept

You Can Lead

Absolute power corrupts, yet so many leaders cling to power like trapeze artists
The trait may be in your DNA or can be acquired by keen learning and observation
Should you have traits of being sociable, bold, assertive or adept at delegation
You may be a lucky natural-born leader; start early, specializing in creative oration

Leadership styles can range from autocratic, laissez-faire, charismatic or visionary
Queen Elizabeth I was an autocrat, in her reign Shakespeare wrote plays legendary
She established Protestantism and made England a rich and prosperous country
A daughter of King Henry VIII, she made the role of leadership look so elementary

Laissez-faire leaders like Steve Jobs and Roosevelt trusted experts to guide them
The Panama Canal and Hoover Dam, creation of Apple Inc, reason for much pride
Napoleon Bonaparte, a charismatic leader, savored how he was followed blindly
The loot of gold he shared with his troops, ensuring his and their focus coincided

Nelson Mandela was a visionary leader, transformed his prison visions into reality
He welded his country, staved off strife, forgave oppressors with a new spirituality
He lit the torch for crusaders of racial freedoms, wrote the rules of a new morality
If you feel the passion and vision of a leader, think of it as a talent, not an abnormality

Grappling with Change

The earth's core, like our minds, is restless and active. Lava still spews profusely
Our mind has lots of nervous energy that keeps us agitated and alert acutely
Tsunamis don't stop, wildfires burn mindlessly, virus and disease consume us
We don't own the planet, can't stop its gyrations, we are caretakers who sustain it

Change is inevitable and ceaseless; we should own it and not be rattled needlessly
We do not decide our birth or death nor sequence our DNA; all just fellow travellers
Respect differences; we didn't create them, let's fight for equality of opportunity
We act selfishly and don't practice community; let's tame our minds to act civilly

Through conservation and embracing climate goals we can prevent a calamity
Of global warming; let's clean the skies and water, keep our minds pollution free
Of tribalism, us versus them, and mindless conspiracy theories, real dangers forsee
God created us, let's love our neighbour, our earth will then be a heavenly marquee

Cleanse our mind of poisoned thoughts that make us chase money and fame
We are merely playing our parts on life's grand stage, let us His kingdom proclaim
The earth will be sustained if we care for it; let's avoid optics, it's no board game
Let not our minds try to control change, let's make brotherliness our trade name

Exercise Body and Mind

My youthful years made me aware of my lackluster physical and mental image
I got a Bullworker exercise device, hoped it would do good for my self-esteem
It took so long to show improved results, I later realized I had a shortfall of protein
Planned to beef up my torso so girls would notice, cut my hair trim like a Marine

My college friends joined a gym and worked on weights, wanting results too soon
Their hearts got damaged, causing physical harm, leaving them sad and marooned
To avoid fatigue don't push too hard, moderation is needed, and be well groomed
Luckily put my head in books and in physical obsession was never ever consumed

Heard of great men like Stalin who did in 20 years what the West did in 200 years
Thought of mastering political stagecraft and got subsumed with a new addiction
Little realizing the brain has a limited capacity to respond to the will, causing stress
Stress is a cause of heart disease and Lupus, which is a disease of a thousand faces

It dawned on me that God created me as well as a few billion brothers and sisters
I began to think global, of hunger and disease, of poverty and destitution figures
Malnutrition in millions of children; they needed a strong mind in a strong body
Obsessed with myself, I have planned to train my thoughts to embody everybody

60 • *Selwyn Almeida*

Jargon

Dad and Mum worked hard, their employers never asked if they had been to college
To make them glad, we filled our craniums with assorted professional knowledge
We studied business to manage companies and law to gain over peer's mileage
All we learned was commercialese and legalese, only this came with this package

This jargon filled us with vanity and made us guardians of its archaic store
We debated puerile differences between extortion and blackmail, null and void
Libel and slander, confidentiality and privacy, assault and battery, statute and law
Plagiarism and copyright, murder and homicide, and this made us men of straw

Business school taught us the differences between bookkeeping and accounting
Accounting and finance, depreciation and amortization, accrual and cash basis
Call and put options, capital and operating lease, shareholders and stakeholders,
Profit and nonprofit, tax and cost base and what was a hostile takeover

This made us a litigious society; we spend our lives and money on these issues
Little do we realize that we need a little common sense to get into our tissues
Honour the Ten Commandments and to your business partners be fair to all
Pay homage to our Creator; instead of worshipping jargon, let's learn to stand tall

62 • *Selwyn Almeida*

Dad Is at Home

Dad came with me to school today; I wondered how he found the time for me
He seemed quiet and subdued, Mum said Dad's job moved to the River Yangtze
I can't fathom who conjured up the plan and left me to sort this emotional debris
Or why we allowed this capital flight or meaninglessly aim for profits predatory

To add insult to injury, my dad is advised to re-school and re-invent himself again
This is Greek and Latin to me and has thrown my dad in a psychological quandary
Mum shows grief; we all pray that God protects us from this evil daylight robbery
To keep our home happy, we need to all call off the bluff of this enforced poverty

Tough times don't last, I am told, an economic spring is bound to re-merge soon
Till I see a renewal, I keep whistling in the dark and wait patiently for a full moon
Our parents deserve better, a steady job bonds their undying love and matrimony
We must pledge to uphold a responsible society and reject the economic baloney

Till Dad is lucky to find a job, even for minimum wage, I will treat him like a king
We have Dad for a reason, and I will pray Mum helps him keep his wedding ring
The bitter money wind blowing is not just about the politics of right and left wing
Let us end the reckless greed so that we can together picnic at the local hotspring

Treasure of Pearls

64 • *Selwyn Almeida*

The Hobo

My office is on a street called Yonge, the bus shelter my executive cabin
My plastic bag is filled with papers, to deal with before each day is done
Passers-by stare, wondering why I dwell so intently on ugly scraps
They soon surmise, and rightly so, I am the hobo who frequents Yonge

My past is hazy, my future bleak, my age is even unknown to me
I remember Mum and Dad when young, so much in love, who made time for me
Mum said the business cycle that did not turn caused my dad to fall
A tumble did he take, and so mighty was the fall that it left no dad for me

The doctors say my brain is harmed by the safety net that broke down with me
I envy nobody that chance raised tall; I just wonder what is wrong with myself
I know wise men that fix rockets well but stand in awe when they stare at me
Until they hopefully unravel this mystery, my office will continue to be on Yonge

The next time perchance you lay your eyes on me, do not be shocked in disbelief
Just live a life of simple piety and enjoy the priceless gifts that comes with love
Virtues are promised if you fear the Lord, and if by chance you become like me
Fear not; in heaven our brains will be fixed by God's angels for all eternity

Lottery

We dream of winning a lottery some day and imagine the heavens opening wide
Making us rich and happy beyond all measure from the gush of the money's tide
Such fatuous notions we harbor, evoking boundless possibilities that never subside
Though we know the road to riches is inheritance or following a work hard guide

It is a harmless little pastime to buy a lotto ticket, after which we begin to daydream
Don't worry that you'll get addicted; playing the game of luck has now gone mainstream
But remember the ticket should be only one, otherwise your life will go downstream
From which you may never recover and may never live to see the fabled Canadian dream

If chance makes you live in penury, do not be alarmed; you can get rich if you read on
Fill your hours assiduously building your character with a good friend and book
Ask the hand of the Creator who on cold and frosty days will blow warm like the Chinook
The Lord will steady your ship of life and you will not have need for grappling hooks

If chance makes you rich, as it will sometimes do, make happy your unfortunate friends
Give more than half to the poor and needy, don't spend it all on just a Mercedes Benz
When your life on earth is done, a warm welcome awaits you and your progeny
The saints will herald your arrival, no need to then dream of being a wealthy wannabe

Paycheck

Dad came home with a winsome smile, Mum reckons he has his paycheck today
It happens twice a month in Toronto, it happened only once a month in Bombay
I plan to tell him my birthday is here and list the expenses he may have to defray
She cautions me; times are not good, downplay the list and maybe go for a buffet

I am too young to understand the cost of living or what salary makes a living wage
My friends in school talk of lavish birthday parties, surely Dad can all this upstage
I will start with Kuwaiti machboos, flavored mutton rice, which is food for a sage
Then have Yemini ginger tea or qisher coffee or on Yemeni halva make a rampage

Maybe thereafter stop for Irani faloodeh vermicelli and Navroz kaloocheh cookies
Or the yummy Syrian kinafa topped with pistachios or else baklava sugar cookies
Lebanese basbousa with desiccated coconut is delicious, as is their meat fatayer
Iraqi dates are on my list, as is Om Ali, which has its Egyptian quintessential flavor

My mother raises her eyebrows and laughs heartily when I reveal my plans
She says dad is no CEO, he's just a janitor and must work now with his hands
I will qualify one day to be a CEO, then I can be paid for work done by my brains
I am Chief Motivational Officer now; I will take Dad one day for a ride on my plane

Treasure of Pearls

Selwyn Almeida

My Bowl

I sit holding my coveted Bowl and gaze at shoppers leaving the grocery store
Some drop pennies and others display their parsimony like the diplomatic corps
Some think I am slothful; that I am not, I bear no grudge, nor their attitude abhor
My mental infirmity makes me dream I was the risen Lazarus at heaven's door

I have heard that wise men talk of the world food security and climate change
I just wish I had a job offering minimum wage rather than sitting looking deranged
Education creates a middle class whose aspirations their incomes cannot sustain
This upward mobility spiral requires acceleration that my brain cannot maintain

If you ever at me sneer, try instead to give, it will provide you a feel-good look
The greatest poets and thinkers had penury mentioned in their life's minute book
Most of you have concentric wants; I have only few needs and wear a gaunt look
The human family needs a bowl of charity, no need to write this in a statute book

Caring for the infirm around you is better than filling the coffers of any charity
They have huge management expense ratios and don't value simple austerity
The global economy has now understood the principle of comparative advantage
Let's learn to give generously when others grieve. It's only in giving do we receive

70 • *Selwyn Almeida*

Misty

Misty the dog trooped in my home one day and eyed me, the dog sitter, intently
Did I pass her litmus test? No confirmation I received. Misty settled in nervously
The next seven days we developed fraternal bonds and I did my tasks with fervency
In doing humble tasks for Misty, I encountered the creator of both Misty and me

Misty wakes up at morn and looks intently at me gorging breakfast in a hurry
Wondering why she can't share the same meal that I consume so furtively
At times, we eat eggs and sausage together, disregarding her advancing infirmity
Alas, Misty's tender digestion runs amuck; reminds me of the Mad Cow malady

Misty has no life game plan or career path, no miles to traverse before she sleeps
No heartaches; she wakes, she eats, and on her housemates' devotion she heaps
After living a dozen years, she will go home, making our hearts to miss a beat
Our loving Creator asks for no life's balance sheet or earnings we made on Wall Street

I could have been Misty and Misty could be me, the Creator plays no favourites
We pine, weep, fear and stress from life's oddities and lack of property rights
When life's cycle takes a turn, or I awake feeling down and forlorn, I think of Misty
Nothing rattled her, content with her bone; it's then when life's mist fades away

Selwyn Almeida

Autumn Colours

The tree leaves outside have changed colour to red, orange, pink, purple and brown
Nature looks ready for a Halloween party or trying on colourful costumes for a prom
The secret does not whisper in the wind but is unraveled in a senior school dorm
The short days of fall makes the chlorophyll in leaves suddenly act lukewarm

In nature there is an unwritten code of spring, summer, autumn and winter in tow
A company also has a life cycle of growth and decline until they move to Mexico
The wrinkles on a human face herald autumn's phase, which no cream can restore
Though the leaves or face lose colour, life still exists, which must be underscored

Admire the changing colours in fall, the beauty and splendor as you jolly along
The mighty winds will soon come upon nature and leave our faces bare and pale
Green the planet and our bodies treat right, its nature's clause in a conditional sale
To this contract let us be true, lest we become targets for our posterity to assail

When faced with an uphill task or dreadful loss, realize green just turned red
It happens in nature year on end, and nature recovers though it appears dead
Let's not drown our sorrows in opioids but uphold our dignity as a thoroughbred
Nature is our life's North Star; fall will pass, let's go and see nature's watershed

Cup of Tea

A cup of tea refreshes most drinkers, its oxidized leaves gives a health boost too
A native plant of China, black tea is drunk in India, which the British introduced
White, green, oolong and black tea are flavorful, and will not an addiction induce
The teenagers have caught on to bubble tea and prefer it over a glass of fruit juice

The long strands of tea from Darjeeling and Assam is first sipped by the Queen
Alphonso mangoes have sugar a plenty; copious tea drinkers be wary of caffeine
On every railway station in the Indian heartland, the tea stall is a familiar scene
Tea with condensed milk boiled in cardamom is standard fare after Indian cuisine

Green tea increases T cells that control inflammation and autoimmune disease
Chamomile tea strengthens immunity; loaded with antioxidants, it surely will please
Tea drinkers are less likely to suffer a stroke or contract cardiovascular disease
If Athenians had just sipped tea, they'd understood the philosophy of Socrates

The Indian premier mastered political stagecraft, learning to sell tea at a stall
Enjoying the cup that cheers, helps battle cancer, and there is no need for cabal
Ginger tea assists digestion, calms nausea, no need to give the office a sick call
It's calorie-free, and by drinking a few cups you may gain expertise at playing hardball

Thrift Stores

The American dream of success we are told is possible to all who may seek it
Sacrifice, hard work and risk-taking, you may be upwardly mobile if you make it
With freedom, equality and opportunity present, bad luck is only yours to blame
Thrift stores and food banks stave disillusionment from your likely elusive fame

While an economic downturn or lack of work may force you to visit a food bank
Visiting thrift stores is smart buying; it's no more the reserve of the urban poor
The well-heeled now realize that you get clothing gems at a fraction of the price
Discard the dubious stigma and join the bandwagon of society's flotation device

While these thrift shops have provided capitalism an ongoing financial lifeline
Teaching poor immigrants to appear as if they were from a renowned bloodline
Stores market a vision statement of hope and service, dignity and stewardship
Ignore these pious banners, among rivals it is just commerce and one-upmanship

For those experiencing hard times or a shoestring budget, thrifting is attractive
Prices have climbed, yet the shopping aisles are packed with an unused clothesline
Burnish your profile and look like Venus or Adonis transported from another time
Salvation needs peace and reconciliation, thrifting avoids economic desperation

Changing Landscape at Work

Large multinationals came to India after the war and paid premium wages
Based on work study, well-paid jobs were not found on employment pages
Exited in the 70s when foreign exchange laws changed the socialist nation
Unscrupulous local investors emerged that caused stakeholder privations

The Arabian Gulf became a magnet for workers who found rewarding work
Money helped migrants build homes, investments were at high watermark
Fabulous wealth made the oil investors park their fortunes in London banks
Accumulations were handy when due to the Gulf War their fortunes tanked

The dot com bubble and banking crisis made USA lose its luster and sheen
Canada stayed a resource economy, investors lost their entire seed capital
Globalization slowed industry, attracting investment fiscally became tactical
Finding good jobs in such a shrinking economy remained at best impractical

The landscape of work has altered the balance in this migration equation
Trained professionals should reconsider mindless flirtation with the West
Jobs are plentiful, now outsourced, stay put at home and avoid depression
Living joyfully with family is better than paying bills here, I must confess

Conspiracy Theories

Vaccinating children can cause autism, children can get disease if you don't
Climate-change science is a hoax, rising seas will inundate us if change is denied
Opinions such as these creates camps whose opposing positions each one derides
Let your conscience be your guide and blame ourselves only for what we decide

Theorists without facts make scapegoats of elites who they blame for social strife
At times the enemy is a group who schemes against the community from outside
Some are conspirators who cannot be recognized but are insidious from within
Some enemies from above manipulate others, folk like us are made to take sides

Conspiracy theories blame coverups for assassinations and government overreach
Make you believe they are coming for your guns and churches; they have global reach
At times amusing when they say Christ never died but went to Kashmir to preach
Assassination of Kennedy was an inside job, truths that were materially breached

These theories are not based on evidence but based on our core beliefs
Examine the evidence and rely on scientists instead of just blind religious beliefs
Zionist are not against Islam, both adherents have abiding faith in one Holy book
Enemies real not imagined, let's be wary, use discernment remain our guidebook

Curve in Your Road

College days lay behind me. In front were dreams of a job, a car and a gentle wife
Energetic, with few skills, and the fact that jobs needed references caused me great strife
Tired of the slow climb, pursued higher studies and hoped it was an elixir of life
Work opportunities improved, made money enough for me, not for a car or wife

Wondered why folks slid into a job and there spent their whole productive life
Enabled them to pay bills, buy sundry assets and stock essential pantry supplies
Few unscrupulous managers exacted hefty kickbacks, some envied and despised
Nepotism and conflict of interest lay shredded, for others it was a pie in the sky

Friends went into business for lack of good employment, not due to special skills
They greased the palms of those who aided their climb up life's prosperity hill
Unreasonable and disallowed expenses creeped into their books; it was a thrill
Taxes got low, profits high, they had fancy cars while we laboured hard in our anthill

There is a curve in everyone's road, when options should be carefully weighed
The master/servant contract brings money in by drips, no big money cascades
You may have to change jobs in your lifetime and at times acquire a good trade
As God's co-creator, the kids need your shade to nurture roots, a slow serenade

Let's Swing Once More

Lower taxes mean more pocket money, but we all need to be gainfully employed
Free market requires the wheels of the economy to be oiled to prevent stalling
Immigration restrictions make good sound bites, but business needs overhauling
Military spending makes economic sense but makes the arms' race look galling

Sensible gun rights are fine in rural areas but in the city, guns are lethal and killing
Abortion restrictions, except in case of rape and incest, would make it less hurting
Union rights make sense with most CEOs, with myopic profit goals they keep flirting
Let's stop being republican, use good sense by being swing voters once more

Protecting the environment helps our planet but needs the world to act in unison
Social safety net helps the vulnerable, but they also need to be loved in person
Universal voting rights are a need, consent cannot be swayed by bots or coercion
Minority rights prevents racial injustice, Christ died for both the Jews and Gentiles

Religious secularism shows love and respect; we must call out fundamentalism
Multiculturalism shows a mature society, but all countries should adopt pluralism
Let's stop being just democrats, use our good sense to be swing voters once more
Party-line voting has stoked hate, swing voting will help all share one dance floor

Global Humanity

Colonial trade took agricultural goods from the East to be processed in the West
Transnational companies emerged and exacted the wages of their prior conquest
The world's brightest were invited to fuel the dot com bubble, a failed plan at best
Globalization arrived, its virtues trumpeted, investors' joy was openly professed

David Ricardo's theory of comparative advantage blossomed as the new gospel
Levitt coined globalization and was the apostle making marketing go full throttle
The aim was to make markets efficient, increase competition and spread wealth
Outsourcing did make the East wealthy, a boost to citizens of the Commonwealth

This led to a period of great excitement, white goods were being sold for a song
Perfect competition delivered the cocktail relished by followers of Mao Zedong
Manufacturing in the West suffered attrition, the dream of good life gone wrong
Buyer's remorse gave way to nationalism, a toxic brew people could not jolly along

The virus left gaping holes in this global plan, national security became a casualty
The health care of countries stood exposed; they had no ventilators or face masks
The Just in Time inventory model failed, the producers of goods were in lockdown
The hymn of globalization needs a pause and reset before the next breakdown

The Giant Sleeps

Canada is an object of other countries' envy, yet Americans don't wish to live here
Vast country, with the largest coastline, that 37 million multicultured people call home
A wonder so large a country holds so few people. Right, bitter cold in the air looms
The worlds 10th largest economy, yet Americans fill up its corporate boardrooms

The far-sighted immigration point-based system is why Canada welcomes the best
118 nationalities have access to good single-payer government healthcare
Affordable colleges, good service jobs, with daycare and childcare, little to despair
40 large parks, the Rocky Mountaineer train is unique, but there's no Times Square

Canadian people have hearts of gold, immigrants and refugees will surely attest,
They gift their property to their children when they get old, no need of a bequest
They have invented hockey and basketball, the lightbulb, insulin and lacrosse
Also, the walkie talkie and the Wonderbra; they love poutine and support the Red Cross

High taxes are matched with high creature comforts, its policies termed socialist
Plentiful agriculture and modern education make it known for its quality of living
They believe in climate change, but have plentiful oil and just can't stop drilling
Love coconut oil, yoga and mindfulness, giving it a character which is so alluring

Channelize Your Thinking

Humankind is part of this existence we share with animate and inanimate objects
Humans are stellar creatures; our brains process thinking that can be complex
Thinking ceaselessly can progress to worry; we need to use some mindful checks
Lest worry spirals out of control, we must be aware of our reality in all respects

Thinking is lively and energizing and pictures our Life, hopes and desires
We investigate our reality and chose to possibly alter it, with some determination
Endeavor to be a good spouse and parent, bringing joy while realizing our aspirations
Let's carefully be aware and accept our reality as it is without craving or aversion

Buddah saw an old man, a sick man and a dead man, and a monk contemplating
The reality set him thinking; he ushered in Buddhism, theories that are pulsating
Through constant prayer let's be divine creatures, preventing evil to permeate
Should our thoughts rattle us or create discomfort, we can these thoughts isolate

Gandhi and Mandela spent time in jail and learned from reading the holy books
That they practice forgiveness, their countries had spectacular order and civility
Mussolini and Hitler thought of enslaving the world; we still talk of their barbarity
Let's channelize our thinking, be creative, bringing all-around enduring prosperity

Cool it Down

The world's great civilizations, like Harappa and Egypt, succumbed to drought
These ancient sites lie buried and appear hibernating in an underground hideout
Climate change, scientists reckon, is a human creation that practical rules flout
It's for humans to fashion a noble bailout, or else all polar bears will be wiped out

The overheated earth can cause extreme weather events and rising sea levels
Retreating glaciers and record temperatures; inaction makes us such daredevils
Ice loss in Antarctica and Greenland makes giant glaciers slide into the ocean
Rising sea levels threaten life on islands; the earth is getting buried in slow motion

Climate-change deniers exist, some recipients of coal-and-oil company funding
Agriculture and health are being harmed, yet protection efforts they are defunding
CO_2 is caused by human fossil-fuel burning, experts agree humans cause warming
Let's invest in renewable energy; it creates more jobs than the fossil-fuel burning

Ocean acidification threatens many food chains, endangering dolphins and whales
Let's address such challenges instead of rooting for margins and higher gross sales
Disaster costs of extreme weather events is rising, looks we have run off the rails
Our will can achieve cuts in warming; we will leave for posterity pristine nature trails

Social Reform

Mother Teresa was asked why she sought band-aid measures, not radical change
She worked for the poor in visual range, felt others could their society rearrange
Reform brings changes like the abolition of slavery and the women's movement
Gradual changes like 'when the floor is dirty, you sweep it' not rip the whole floor

India was lucky to have Baba Amte, who worked to rehabilitate leprosy patients
Mohan Roy crusaded against Sati, or bride burning, which shook people's complacence
Ambedkar championed the uplift of poor castes, which did away with slavish obeisance
Vinoba Bhave showed the power of silence and fasts in his fight for human rights

True, such changes did not fundamentally change the society in which people lived
Harriet Tubman, a black American abolitionist, led scores of Blacks to emancipation
Martin Luther King Jr. fought for civil rights when white privilege was a fixation
Abraham Lincoln steered the antislavery drive, and freedom found a new foundation

The social and religious reforms attacked bigotry, superstition and oppression
Today we hear the clarion call for women's rights, gay rights and voting rights
The reformers analyzed shortcomings of their society and set high their sights
The prophets came to remind us of our better angels and that humans reunite

The Indian Thali

Thali, a steel circular Indian dish, with a cluster of katoris, provides a balanced diet
It could be made of dazzling copper, if you want to be a cut above the proletariat
Dal and beans in the sambar tickle your olfactory nerves not your tastes prurient
Which comes from animal fat, the vegetarian thali is a nontoxic diet and luxuriant

Tropical vegetables, organic and colourful, fill the thali, you could start with puris
The rice and dals, rasam and sambar, may lead you to postprandial somnolence
Diabetics be warned, rice causes sugar spikes, insomniacs need not take sedatives
Sleep is a natural cure for the bodys aches, the food is free from bad carcinogens

The Indian thali has taken the world by storm, many have added meat to the fare
Indian spices in vegetarian food, namaste and yoga are now a triangular fanfare
Dieticians promote vegetarian meals, food chains be mindful of your market share
You need not be a Hindu to learn yoga or eat vegetarian, it's enlightened healthcare

Vegetarian food is easy to digest, soft on the gut, you can stave off diverticulitis
The thali provides a standard healthy alternative to food that can be indigestible
No avian, swine flu or mad cow virus to deal with, also saving endangered species
To conserve the planet and remain healthy, let's all go try the famous Indian thali

Selwyn Almeida

Happy Andy

Andy was a charming teen, smiled from ear to ear. I was privileged to be his friend
Born with no silver spoon, reasons for his magnetism were difficult to comprehend
His dad worked two jobs, Mum at home, valiantly trying to tie their lives' loose ends
While other boys sought a girlfriend, Andy stayed true to his society of friends

He wished all well, never compared himself to others on whom dame luck smiled
Never dreamed of winning a lottery, no problems that life threw ever made him rile
He complimented your looks and attire, he appeared to be like the Lily of the Nile
Couldn't afford college and joined the army and was loved by both rank and file

The wise say happiness results from good health, bad memory and enjoying a nap
Life is not perfect but being able to see beyond it weathers life's many cold snaps
Money does not make you happier, relationships do; surely Andy would agree too
The unhappy derive comfort from seeing others sad, Andy would such thoughts eschew

I am grateful to Andy, thank my maker for giving me this friendship dividend
Enemies of happiness are pain and ennui, but Andy such pitfalls sought to transcend
When you get sad and restless, think of Andy – he had the same issues to contend with
Chose to be happy, his laughter was infectious; Andy's character had no split ends

The Joker

The solitary joker in a deck of cards at times assumes the role of the kingmaker
In our teens, we too begin to see a joker in us, and this becomes an image breaker
Our inner joker unhappy with the shape of our nose, face and colour of our skin
Realizing our unique strengths, let's resolve to from a joker become a kingpin

At school some friends are smart, some athletes, and others talented musicians
Basking in the glory of success, while we wonder what ails our life's slow ignition
Some friends are lucky; others pursue solid careers with their brains' ammunition
Wonder how to calibrate our life or solve simple math and avoid mental attrition

History is replete with tales of people who had little and yet rose from the ashes
Gandhi and Mandela found fame later in life, Steve Jobs' luck came in patches
Jesus and Buddha, like other prophets, have helped us retrieve our life from ashes
All played the joker in their lives, but their message survived their bodies' gashes

When feeling lost, or if friends and relatives desert you, recall the joker in the pack
You won't be down long; you the Joker will emerge, a gallant knight on horseback
The cynosure of all eyes, avoid being a megalomaniac or have an anxiety attack
So, to steer the ship of life or steady a business, it's nice to be a joker in the pack

Divorce is Avoidable

A breezy romance, whirlwind honeymoon, exchange of rings, I imagined love ever after
Life's flawless mirror cracked, what happened suddenly, I found out two summers later
Cement and sand mixed makes concrete; we discreetly realized we were incompatible
Conflicts grew from differing opinions, neighbors felt love had lost all its working capital

Humans are amorous creatures, seeking greener pastures with mates their eyes behold
Thought marriage would slow down the dating speed, infidelity somehow took a foothold
Till they are caught, throw caution to the winds, enjoying prurient pleasures all blindfold
Faithfulness is marriage's spinal cord; divorce is sought when passions aren't controlled

You may have reckoned when marrying that your partner would stay a golden goose
The Midas touch of the married couple could weather all calamities that ever let loose
When the money dries, love dissipates and is replaced with alcohol or substance abuse
These are grounds for a legal divorce; money does matter, in marriage you will deduce

Marriage was meant to be a sacrament till death do us depart, kids need Dad and Mum
The sanctity of marriage is lost with incompatibility, infidelity or erosion of family income
Carefully consider all these three cardinal rules before you to love's ecstasy succumb
Dating years are time to ponder how divorce can flatten the taste of heady Jamaican rum

Relatives

Mum and Dad, Grandpa, Grandma, sisters and brothers I knew to me were related
Relatives add up with marriage and adoption, your small world is now populated
At birthdays, christenings and anniversaries you meet them and may feel elated
Such associations were caused by chance, which at times needs to be tolerated

You will befriend people by design who are like you in character or disposition
Children of doctors band together; the jargon is understood, as are their positions
On fees paid tardily to their parents and total rejection of all alternative medicine
Kids of factory workers are no exception; they agree it's time for wage expansion

The Holy Book exhorts us to love our neighbour as our self, by goodwill and respect
Many wonder why it's hard to love relatives whose actions you at times detest
Condescending occasionally, imposing their worldview or putting you to an acid test
Of compliance, which is difficult to digest; your mind seems as in a house arrest

Relatives who rarely judge others or seek a speck in other's eyes practice humility
It pays off to be courteous and respectful to all, it advances peace and harmony
Anger, holding a grudge, or revenge and retaliation are qualities of the battlefield
Plan to be a friendly relative; you will then experience love's gravitational field

Slowing Down

The raging tempest of emotions subsides and has taken the wind from my sails
My mind was a hammer and everything was a nail; now bare wisdom prevails
The mind and body are robbed of vitality, leaving you overwhelmed by this change
This slowing down can be disarming, nature now acting as a commodity exchange

The roaring forties find you at the zenith of your career, friends your ego feed
Your star shines and a halo of invincibility appears over you like a string of beads
Prone to make errors of judgment that you may regret, wild emotions to blame
Money in the pocket, your whim to feed, nature slowly begins its waiting game

The somber fifties fill you with cares and worries of children and unfinished tasks
Nature, an honest broker, plays by a swap of a contentment mask for vitality lost
Desire no more will be your mistress that tormented your soul since your teens
Live and let live will be your motto and you will enjoy peace like marines come to shore

It's time to slow down and catch the whiff of the breeze caressing your cheek
Time to take a book or spend time with friends and family, or just say a prayer
The Lord is merciful, and to receive his abundant blessings, let's touch base with him
The fifties slows and steadies you, yet before old age sets in, let's enjoy the prelims

Selwyn Almeida

The Walker

Your gentle frame the walker draws, your eyes transfixed at the door
Looking intently, I wonder if my visit will fructuous be, or will fate deny
Luckily, I gaze and see the gleam of joy abound when our eyes met in embrace
My soul surrendered, my spirits soared, and to the heavens I bent in silent praise

None can dream what life for them has stored, or chance doth ordeals bring
But ingratitude hurts the sensitive soul; the walker can never guess nor restore
The tube helps you wade through life, no shore except heaven can you see
Only faith tempers the saddened soul; my visit at most can only small mercies bring

I wish Dad were there today to provide you comfort in your advancing age
He may have honoured his marriage pledge he made to you with his youthful gaze
Little did you conjure the children born of such sweet and noble dreams
Would abandon thee, pursuing fatuous personal dreams of elusive bliss

The book of life and the rosary beads for your tortuous soul some respite brings
The walker remains your faithful friend, and some sanity and mobility provides
You bear no hurt, no vengeance feeds your soul, faith such serenity brings
Though the end is near, your life reminds us to love as God loves us ungrateful souls

The Empty Room

The children have grown, gone to pursue their dreams, the home turns so silent
The furniture has no one to laze on; it's an eerie quiet in a place once so vibrant
The beds look tidied, like a hotel room for no purpose; the kids are now migrants
Let's offer bed and breakfast, after adding some essential home refinements

Starry-eyed when married, the kids came along soon, complete with assignments
Preparing breakfasts, lunches and dinners, appeared like solitary confinement
Kids' chores made our marriage appear like society's device of marital entrapment
Executed tasks with deft and precision, no time to read Maugham or Maupassant

The parenting game changes at the teens, wonder whether they inherited your genes
Contain yourself, if you feel this way, esteem issues arise if you spill all the beans
Rides to their games, doctors and friends will turn you into a chauffeuring dean
At prom, be sure to call them queens, even if their dresses were not dry-cleaned

Such tasks we laboriously endure, and we oddly miss the kids when they suddenly go
Should this make you an empty-nester feel, time to make a trip to Rio de Janerio
Make a bucket list or trace the steps of Somerset Maugham in the Malay Archipelago
If your funds run dry, do not be alarmed, try your dame luck at the Spanish lotto

Thanksgiving Day

Lincoln taught us to appreciate the blessings of fruitful fields and healthful skies
We thank God for a bountiful harvest as well as family ties we seek to optimize
So, while we indulge in turkey, caviar and french fries, let's not the poor despise
There are over 40 million food-insecure homes here, to no one's surprise

Families need affordable housing, a good education and nutrition, let's empathize
True joy comes from sharing and lifting our brothers, let no one get desensitized
Hard times help us increase not diminish our faith, let's like one leper be grateful
Ingratitude is an overlooked habit, the tooth of the winter wind is not so unkind

Let's not entangle ourselves in the weeds of materialism, lust of success or fame
The holy book asks us not to be anxious about anything, but pray and be grateful
God will not forsake you, do not lean on your own understanding but be prayerful
Let's look after each other, true thanksgiving will then become a value universal

Let us pray for our devout and self-sacrificing parents, our teachers and siblings
Let's pull down walls and get rid of nuclear weapons; they are lethal and killing
Thank our reformers who espouse equality and stir our hearts, however unwilling
When we have racial and gender equality, that thanksgiving will be truly thrilling

96 • *Selwyn Almeida*

The Evergreens

Oh mighty winter, mistake not your strength, your villainy makes the world pause
Your breath is harsh and cruel, and men and beast cower at your tyrannical paws
Huddle in their homes to stay warm and thus submit to your indomitable strength
Only the smiling evergreen stands tall and unbowed, keeping you at arm's length

Oh evergreen, what pact exists with nature that you withstand winter's ravages
Your needle-shaped leaves, such formidable armour, display as a well-oiled engine
Your conical face displays grit, not beauty; no flowers on your tall torso reside
Yet you fight the odds by resilience and take harsh winter all in your stride

Oh man, why do life's vicissitudes throw you in disarray and your nerves fray?
Knowing that ravages of winter are nature's minor blemish, spring heralds joy
Troubles with time dissipate, knowing the evergreen with fortitude wins the day
So, with endurance and prayer, steady your life's ship, to demons never fall prey

Oh God, why are humans, your stellar creature, not as strong as the evergreen?
With minor life's twists and turns expresses sadness as though they have no spleen
Suffer untold misery at a change of circumstance or turn of fortune's wheel
Let him be brave as the evergreen and not succumb and fold up like chow mein

Tolerance

Personal tolerance for prodigal sons, wayward daughters and spouses is known
Is it stigma, ridicule or narcissism that domestic oddities are willingly condoned?
We must try to tolerate people whose colour, race and opinions, which many abhor
Tolerance is a bulwark against prejudice, ignorance and hatred in life's bigoted store

The underlying basis of tolerance is respect for the beliefs and practices of others
Truth is relative, our beliefs too; let's be pleasant, calm and a patient brother too
You will enjoy health and peace and will also not violate others' inalienable rights
The Good Lord tolerates our many faults; let's show others our merciful flashlight

Tolerance has limits; we have hate laws to curb our spiteful, bellicose ignorance
Tolerance limits are used in engineering to control physical dimension variance
Intolerance has no place in religion; it is caused by ignorance and indoctrination
Fundamentalism is seen as an effect of globalization – avoid nefarious associations

Mideastern hotheads did not know their religious beliefs had a common origin
Gay and straight is not a choice to stray, but in our DNA; its no American invention
Desert folk wearing black flowing gear – don't call them penguins, it's racial profiling
We are redeemed by His suffering on the Cross, a pedagogy so true and defining

Love Will Calm Fear

Lead us on, precious Lord, lead us home to the light, we have sadly strayed
O Shepherd of Sheep, open our eyes and lead us to the path of enlightenment
Verily I say to you, to all who believe in love, that it will lead you to everlasting life
Enjoy the harvest; the fruits are in such abundance, let's leave no one behind

We have parents to guide our paths and a constitution to be our steady north star
Independents among us, you hold the key; help bring us to shore when we drift
Legal minds among us, remind and help us respect the letter and spirit of the law
Love, which is selfless, be held out to be our only adjudicator when we have a tie

Curse not those with whom you differ; respect is a sign of grace and civility
Attack not the people who do not look like you; the cross redeemed us all
Lecture not what you think is right or wrong; the greatest minds have evolved
Mend your evil ways. Let the sun not go down on your wrath, reckoning is near

Fear of economic and cultural insecurity can be replaced by faith and prayer
Enjoy nature's diversity, Noah was told to take one of each kind into his big boat
Aaron led a great army but was defeated; love and faith are the best generals
Respect and rejoice our differences. Love and compassion are an antidote to fear

Forty Days in Lent

Ash Wednesday begins a period of reflection with the goal of self-purification
Gone is Pancake Tuesday and carnival preceding Lent; feels like it's now deflation
Personal alienation results from doing things we don't wish to, creates frustration
Lenten quiet, prayer and fasting renews the spirit, as sacrifice is good for the soul

Adam and Eve are believed to have disobeyed God and eaten the forbidden apple
When confronted about their lapse, they hid their nakedness behind fig leaves
Most of us suffer alienation when we hide our faults instead of coming out clean
Lent is a time to look inwards, feel sorry and ask forgiveness, a moral sunscreen

Some give up alcohol, some abstain from chocolate; it's good for body and soul
When tempted to call the discipline off, think of the collapsed star and blackhole
It's easy to fold – look at the New Year resolutions: all have by now fallen in a pothole
Lent's forty days of sacrifice and reflection is uplifting, like shooting a solo field goal

Fasting purifies the body and the soul, it is a pillar in Islam, a moral act for Hindus
Yom Kippur is set aside by Jews as a period of atonement. Lent creates avenues
For spiritual renewal; atheists, don't be bemused, take the occasional moral cruise
Denying few pleasures of the body enhances self-esteem and is real good news

Leisurely Retirement

Lucky people retire after years of hard work and soon realize happiness is elusive
The family money well dries up, loneliness and boredom creep if you are reclusive
The mind takes over the steering wheel, swerving round roadblocks of negativity
Christ and the martyrs died early, so let's enjoy life and stay away from passivity

Exercise, bathe regularly to stay healthy; the body disintegrates surely but rapidly
Simple meals of lentils and vegetables must be on the table, eat meat randomly
Relax when you see the pace of life is slow, read a book and often visit the library
Gardening makes you a junior botanist, or just watch a film like When Harry met Sally

Financial planners appear like angels, asking us to plan for the uncertain future
Should you have a problem of plenty, they will an attractive estate plan suture
Most simple folk don't fit in such shoes, stay with family, be a trooper to their kids
Or maybe just structure a simple reverse mortgage; it makes a good landing skid

The morning alarm now stops, you don't have to be a slave or foolishly worry
Changes in a company's life cycle, or in the boss, no longer makes your eye blurry
It's time to frolic and have fun, or share with friends your famed chicken curry
You ran the race as best as you could, it's time to relax and enjoy life's snow flurry

The Cross Never Goes Away

Ever since my teenage years, I remember being weighed down with my little cross
Dad became union boss; his alcohol addiction grew around us all like an albatross
Mum laboured to hold us tight, heroism that deserved a distinguished service cross
I then turned to Jesus, who weathered storms; he too had carried his heavy cross

Jesus propagated a new religion: love the stranger and care for the downtrodden
Seen as a threat to the social elite and Roman nation, he cared for the forgotten
They crucified him; punishment so savage that Emperor Constantine then banned
Jesus never complained; he carried his cross, an end to our troubles we demand

We buy a lottery ticket, we work, love and marry and hope in life we do get lucky
We soon realize that's wishful thinking; things soon fall apart, thoughts look fuzzy
Wonder why our cross doesn't go away. You recall Jesus too tried to wish it away
Carry it boldly, this infirmity no substance abuse can take away, it's here to stay

Many feel fame and fortune are elusive and they are solitary souls being tossed around
Humankind is like peas in a pod, troubles are varied, it bears all of us down
Help others carry their cross, comforting words dispels fears and calm all down
Even for folks who have privileges from cradle to grave, the cross is always around

Canadian Refugee Migrants

Suffering displacement and persecution, thousands requested a Canadian home
We are humane and welcoming, not due to an order from the Church of Rome
Loneliness can be crushing; it's refreshing when someone opens wide their door
Canada wipes your tears, and requests for asylum and safe harbor will not ignore

Immigration keeps the economy buoyant and staves of any impending recession
Regular migrants come with skills and the cash; they are tolerated as a concession
The entry of refugees send some into a tailspin and puts this policy to a question
Refugee success stories, if heard, would have surely reduced this naked aggression

The Syrian confectioners and shawarma shops are a testament to their resilience
The Vietnamese boat people are now professionals with careers that are brilliant
The Afghan fruit and vegetable vendors makes Downsview Flea Market a pavilion
Most came as refugees; they are law abiding and pay taxes running into millions

Our religious values prescribe we show kindness to strangers and the forgotten
Opening doors to refugees appears reckless but is a sound economic argument
The majority of Canadian people are truly compassionate, to which refugees attest
Let Canada remain a North Star to all nations; it has passed life's tough road test

Love is Commitment

I love my mother, I love eating shrimp and I love ogling beautiful women
I soon realize one is concern, the other is pleasure and the last stems from lust
Innocent activities require applying brakes to prevent you getting cussed
In fact, I attempt to escape from loneliness and feel the need for affection

Committed love shows kindness and affection, loyalty is the gold standard
Spending time, sharing big moments, able to prioritize, love finds an anchor
Understanding the value of commitment, you are now a clever Love Banker
Your investments will yield dividends, your discussions will be rich in candor

Mutual love and no commitment are a burst of passion, soda minus the fizz
A youthful pleasure requiring maturity, informed consent, a reckless fling
Its seeds thrown on rock, enjoyed by vultures who treat you like a plaything
If heartaches arrive, take it with ease; it was passion made on a box spring

Marriage is not just a social contract, it derives from love and commitment
You must be willing to play your part and cement bonds to make it resilient
Children come and bring joy and work; you now are parents to your infants
When marriage bells toll, think very hard and don't be passive or indifferent

Brother's Keeper

World War I killed 20 million; the reasons for this war are varied and elusive
Twenty years later, World War II killed 65 million, hatred turned explosive
We had not learned lessons, our hearts grew cold, at times looked frozen
We should have been brothers in God's nation, our love wide as the ocean

Though scattered across the globe, we are all bound in common humanity
Tribalism and racial prejudice expose our mean-mindedness and insanity
Let us be brothers and each other's keeper, our core remaining philanthropy
We can end wars by calling our Creator Father and act as one royal family

The Spanish Flu killed 40 million, HIV claimed the lives of 36 million brothers
We could act in unison, cooperate and collaborate to eliminate all disease
Our hearts must beat for even one soul gone before time, we hold the key
A tragedy in Japan, China or Antarctica is a human problem, let's all agree

The Chernobyl disaster or the Exxon oil spill remind us of human safety
The coronavirus should have been handled by us collectively and bravely
The oceans separate our continents, but God binds us with his fatherly love
Bind us together, Lord, bind us together with bonds that cannot be broken

Proverbial Parent

The marriage journey starts with a lot of love and a small dose of commitment
Couples are rarely mentally prepared for children storming into their lives
The first child brings anxiety; the parents are novices with very few skills
Overnight you are now providers – can we find someone to dispel our chills

For the first time we realize the sacrifices our parents took to raise us up
The holy book exhorts each one of us to honour our father and mother
A wise son makes a glad father, but a foolish son is a sorrow to his mother
Daughters need training to love their husbands and children, joy it ushers

Welcome brief relief comes with kids gone to start their lives, joy ensues
Parents suddenly experience an empty nest, their wedding vows must renew
Stay-at-home parents struggle, let go, and new activities must now pursue
Boomerang kids at times come home, needing to be carefully attended to

Some women enjoy the peace of mind and stability an empty nest brings
Men stay married, serenity comes with tugging your wife's apron strings
The Japanese believe you must possess "Ikigai," which is a purpose in life
If you cannot unravel a purpose, it's okay, just be good husbands and wives

A Roof over Your Head

It may be a thatched roof, tin roof, owned or rental roof above your head
The incessant rain and howling winds do not intimidate the wed or unwed
A wise investment, don't by joys of immediate gratification ever be misled
Silver and gold may be gilt edged, but a roof protects both body and soul

Bella and Bobsy were gentle folk who had no kids dancing on their porch
Returned from Africa with four trunk loads, their lives and finances torched
Couldn't find a job, they auctioned their belongings that were in their box
It went on till they got bone dry; for want of a roof, they bore life's shocks

Relatives well-meaning ventured to help but soon questioned their judgement
Philanthropy was not one of their virtues; relations sour, turn ugly and pungent
Many migrants will attest how their host's rules of eating turned too stringent
Invest in a roof before relations get frigid, it's part of your wise due diligence

When you get old, children seek out your fortune and try to gain a foothold
Train them to have a good education, and a roof on their head is green gold
Bella and Bobsy would have been happy if these life's lessons to them were told
Parents instill character by example, one being to have a roof over their head

Sound Moral Judgements

Religious signposts are egregiously scattered since our birth on our life's roadmap
Instructions divinely ordained are to be maintained when you are a grown-up man
Death sometimes precedes with intense pain, false compassion can't be the plan
Cultured men call for death with dignity, the inner voice says you are a strawman

Christ, when on the cross, asked his father earnestly why He had forsaken him
He foresaw his death, death on the cross, but never sought to alter his destiny
In suffering we are called on to suffer patiently, knowing it instils in us endurance
Physician-assisted dying is an attack on the soverignity of God, so don't surrender

These religious signposts afford little place to use discernment and compassion
Contraception, called a licence turning into licentiousness, now is in high fashion
Same-sex couples are an attack on God's plan of procreation, it's such a distraction
Dying with dignity is violating God's law; there is no place for affirmative action

Reason and careful discernment should step into the place filled by blind dogma
Freedom movements called for independence, which was the call of the Mahatma
Let's disengage and not fear scripture when a strong compassionate case emerges
Perspectives of good, honest people deciding differently is not worthy of scourges

True Sonship

We swear by the constitutional right of equality, good, it's not just an article of law
Many of our brothers feel they are not treated equal – is equality then just hoopla?
Harijans in India, Indigenous People of Canada, natives and racially black America
All realize justice promised has not arrived for them, part of any ecclesiastical law

The constitution enacted in India, Canada and America enacted equality for all
The courts understood it; the good news was propagated 2000 years ago by St. Paul
Custom and tradition then meant loving one another, was limited to close family
Pontification of ideals must move to true justice espoused by the Sage of Gallilee

Positive affirmation laws raised the status of Harijans, people slowly came along
Civil Rights Act in America promised justice; social tensions exist, struggle is lifelong
Natives in America experience prejudice, wrongly treated as lazy and sub-human
Till we all mend our hearts and minds, it will be a rough ride for our fellow crewmen

Men and women of faith, revisit the holy books; God came for all, no exclusions
Others, examine your human values, don't accept injustice and remain delusional
Love of God and abiding human values must make us adopt equality and justice
No amount of codified law can repair this social problem; let God remain our Judge

Solidarity Marches On

We are one family in this world's sprawling tent; let none of us sleep hungry,
Let not bigoted men teach you otherwise, don't ride on their selfish buggy
Barns are full to feed all, the Good Lord will replenish our depleted inventory
Teach cultivation to all, share high-yielding seeds; love makes fertile ground

Healthcare is not the preserve of only the few, it's a universal article of faith
Don't hide behind false pretenses of affordability, let our greed now modulate
Vaccines and medicine are a right of all; let no one your thoughts manipulate
Quality of life is a mantra not of anarchists, but believers who think straight

Choice of occupation is based on innate skills, not due to practice of exclusion
Christ was a good teacher, affordable education should be our sole obsession
Education opens our eyes to wisdom and understanding, lessens aggression
Three cornerstones increase our social worth; let's legislate now, not vacillate

We are God's creatures, black, brown, white, yellow, different only in shades
All endowed with God-given precious talents, which has made us a jack-of-all-trades
We can together weather all storms; God watches over us with a fatherly gaze
Heaven has arrived. Welcome it in. From religious bigotry let's stay unfazed

Judgement

Mums willingly love and embrace their babies and thus their indelible bond grows
She sings you nursery rhymes and lullabies, pure thoughts that won't decompose
She wishes you scale glass ceilings in your career and pride on the family bestow
Never would she want to see you kill people so heartlessly with a gun or crossbow

God fashioned each one of us in his own image and likeness; he is father to us all
He loves even those whose faith hasn't matured, built with us no Chinese walls
Should anyone to you whisper, hate your brother or render him false judgement
Reject evil from friends, family or impious holy man, as these are toxic to the soul

Old-fashioned religion is the basis of our laws that we see in our statute books
It encourages love and mercy to all; this is part of Loving God's own pocketbook
We must practice this even on them whose faith we don't share, nor their outlook
Let history remind us of your nobility, not your links with your bigoted hood

On Judgement Day, our life's balance sheet, will angels place before our Father
God will ask to count people you touched with love, not who you slaughtered
The world is big, and many truths are beyond our grasp, let God be the judge
We are in this earthly ship together, let's trust in God and not on worldly fudge

Angelic Values – Hope and Faith

My neighbours placed food on the windowsill for crows, their dad had passed away
Instead of crows, two angelic birds, Hope and Faith, appeared, much to their dismay
Their anguish turned to enlightenment, the birds' chatter took their breath away
Hope and Faith sang of angelic values the world needs; they weren't just birds of prey

Hope, she assisted those in poverty, sickness, and captivity; life is otherwise burdensome
People will not readily bear pain without her – where there is Life there is Hope
The Hope lane, she warns, is long but is a panacea for disease, disaster and sin
For the lost, forgotten and distraught she binds mind and body like a safety pin

Faith, she sang while reason was the left hand of the soul, she was its right hand
She was the substance of things hoped for, the evidence of things not easily seen
Painted as stoking, betting, speculation, when she really provided assurance serene
Faith needs good works, reforms sinners, heals the sick, acts as a moral sunscreen

The neighbour's kids pledged to take care of their mum, then the crows' caw was heard
Hope and Faith are angels to be welcomed by us hapless souls, they cannot be caged
Love of our neighbour is an article of Faith, let's collaborate, not remain disengaged
The angelic birds spread comfort and joy, and only with good works we will be gauged

Healthy Living

The Galilean paid the price for preaching equality by being hanged to a cross
His message was the Love of God and neighbour, should we in our hearts emboss
He was a good teacher who spoke in parables for the simple folk to understand
He gave sight to the blind, cured infirmities; he understood health care firsthand

Keeping robust our bodies and mind as well needs to be part of any social plan
It's an investment in our people; let us in this fight be one another's point man
When we die, our life's work will lay bare whether you read the Bible or Koran
Universal healthcare is a capsule of our faith; while some suffer, let's not look on

Earth is home to countless living things, it is all part of our loving God's master plan
Our earth we must protect, and our rivers and ozone layer are nobody's trashcan
Global warming, greenhouse gases must be eliminated not by measures arcane
Let's invest in healthcare and climate change, the Galilean's death was not in vain

A healthy body and planet sustains our souls, let's not chose to at times to debate
Dinner tables needs to embrace health urgency and sterile debate checkmate
Our neighbours and environment are our religious mission and personal mandate
Let's elect officials who care for our planet and not these noble thoughts berate

Inheriting Your Genes

Medical study has enabled us to understand the mystery of life, not its purpose
DNA contains genes, a unit of heredity, held with a thread called chromosomes
The symmetry of CTAG in the DNA is as pivotal as the part played by hormones
Changes in the CTAG symmetry causes genetic disorders, still a creepy unknown

Replication of the 21st chromosome causes Down's syndrome and cognitive delay
Thalassemia limits production of hemoglobin, cystic fibrosis block your airways
Sickle cell anemia blocks blood vessels, causes organ damage and general malaise
Genetic mutations are inherited, at times through smoking, sun's rays and X- rays

Genetic inheritance disorders can be heart disease, high blood pressure, diabetes
Alzheimer's disease, cancer, arthritis and obesity mire easily the human species
Parents can take a carrier genetic test; it will calm and caution you, a unique key
Forewarned is forearmed, parents look for healthy kids, results are not guaranteed

If you are born genetic disease free, avoid the sun, x-rays, tobacco and chemicals
Environmental factors can mutate your genes; this is well known and chronicled
Mum's genes account for our temper, intelligence, migraines – it's phenomenal
Daughters get their good looks from their father, they may look like Lucille Ball

Autoimmune Disorders

Blood is thicker than water, you hear, but are seldom told it is a warrior for you
Red cells from the marrow of the bone ferries bodily nutrients like a courier crew
Lymph glands makes white cells, which disable germs on whom an antidote spew
When the white immune cells are confused, they attack the body and a fight ensues

The immune fight in the pancreas, which creates insulin, leads to type 1 diabetes
Lack of insulin can damage your eyes, nerves, and cause cardiovascular disease
Rheumatoid arthritis results when the immune system attacks joints and knees
It causes redness, warmth, soreness and stiffness and is such a mental tease

Multiple sclerosis results when nerve cells of the nervous system are attacked
It causes numbness, weakness, balance and walking issues, which is matter of fact
Systemic lupus appears as a skin disease; it affects organs that need to be tracked
Crohn's disease inflames the GI tract, our warrior cells stop keeping nature's pact

Autoimmune disease can leave doctors flummoxed, they must not be blamed
An antinuclear antibody- ANA blood test reveals issues that need to be contained
A high-fat, high-sugar diet is sometimes blamed, the truth is still not ascertained
Absence of immune woes is no birthright, during which we must humor maintain

Treasure of Pearls

The Digestive Puzzle

The fire gets lit each morning. Coconut coir slowly ignites the wooden firewood
In earthenware pots rice is cooked first, then coconut fish curry and vegetables
The well water, spices, coconut and fresh fish fills the air with a magical aroma
At noon they say the angelus sit for their meal. Haven't heard of mad cow disease

Meat was eaten only on Sunday, purchased from the butcher outside the church
People lived long lives, and the calories they consumed ensured they stayed trim
There were also people who consumed wildlife, mongoose and wild boar
Digestive tracks fashioned for plant food ran amok and caused viruses and disease

Eating meat in moderation, well cooked, tickles our tastebuds and satisfies cravings
The human species have become adventurous and now consume exotic wildlife
Rodents, birds, snakes, pangolins and bats, a heady cocktail dish filled with viruses
Consuming red meat improperly cooked is as gory as killing sharks for their fins

Viruses jumping from animals to humans is a logical straight and natural path
We have no devices to eliminate their savage destruction of poor human bodies
Running after a cure while the viruses replicate is like catching the bull by the tail
Let's modify our eating habits, eat right, stop the virus, and end its destructive trail

Mastering Work and Destiny

Flashbacks of my childhood years bring back to me fond memories of little Sadru
Emaciated, just 8, Sadru was brought to work for a local hotelier from Tamil Nadu
His dad was happy to make a verbal contract, terms Sadru had not consented to
He toiled to keep the restaurant clean, his course of destiny only the gods knew

Early morning the scrubbing of the floors was priority; Sadru did this on his knees
Smiling at his destiny, he cleaned the hotel tables before breakfast patrons arrived
Sadru would wash glasses, plates, no time to rest, never thought he was deprived
Occasionally cutting potatoes, onions; his smile had patrons amazed and electrtrified

Every evening at 6 he would emerge and befriend us, children of his tender age
He told us of guests who fawned at his skills and said he would be someone big
He mastered the art of meet and greet and knowing what is profit and loss
Luck is when preparation meets opportunity; he hoped he would one day be a boss

The owner's son fell in bad company, Sadru offered his skills to revive the business
Dame destiny entered his life, the owners soon loved Sadrus strategy and vision
He was promoted as manager, the patrons seconded the plan, hard work paid off
Sadru is a master now of his destiny; life's upsides and downsides are a giant tradeoff

Endure the Cold Snaps

Canada as an immigrant destination is being marketed aggressively by newcomers
Universal healthcare and bilingual education are ideal ground to pursue
choice careers
Paid maternity and paternity leave; with safety and security, there is little to fear
Free speech is tempered with hate-speech laws, your character no one can smear

The winters are short but cold, New Yorkers would never wish to settle over here
Majority of the polar bears live here; it's home to fresh-water lakes greatly revered
You should dress for the weather, lest you notice frostbite on your skin appear
The howling winter winds can be cold, yet people are warm and love to drink beer

People are gracious and kind and instead of a good morning say "Sorry" all the time
They are open to pot and homosexuality, and there is not much organized crime
They enjoy democracy, and ethics violations are debated as a national pastime
At times provinces threaten secession, the confederacy has weathered bad times

Welcoming to immigrants, as they shore up the precarious agricultural economy
The newcomers bring money, skills and talents both technical and gastronomic
You should enquire about immigration downsides, which can be socioeconomic
No one tells you these; they believe there will be warm summers after a cold snap

Takeovers

Love is blind, as lovers will attest to; the emotional takeover comes unplanned
The world of money is scheming, companies encounter backhanded takeovers
Forward and backward integration are at times the cause, or just a tax rollover
Cash-rich companies or sleeping beauties are a prize much sought in a takeover

Companies run by summer soldiers – directors who willingly consent to the raid
Overtures start at times with a bear hug, letter friendly in tone, nuance is weighed
Can start with a creeping takeover, early dawn raid, a no-holds-barred free trade
Shark watchers like analysts and lawyers supposed to keep watch feel dismayed

Lovers get traumatized with the loss of their bride to a rich or an elegant suitor
Wonder if strategy could help this event stave; it's hard to find a good love tutor
Astute owners use golden parachutes or lobster traps, radar alerts or safe harbor
Neuter the raider with a poison pill or shark repellants, now part of one's armour

All is fair in love and war; owners use a scorched-earth policy or just sandbagging
Cleverly introduce a supermajority amendment or go for a bootstrap acquisition
This is the jargon of mergers and acquisitions; you can make it your life's mission
Perfect the role of a hired gun with a killer bee ambition, your useful ammunition

Navigating Controls

Managers run companies they don't own, for oversight owners appoint auditors
Cost, management and financial control are deployed to prevent fraud if it occurs
Budgets and forecasts all assume working controls, steadying the sunshine years
Fraudsters emerge in disguise of overzealous entrepreneurs or complicit auditors

Unless the company is a cash cow or a star, controls are very difficult to maintain
At the end of the life cycle, assets need to be sold, generating only a capital gain
If setting personal controls, be mindful of roadblocks like age and financial terrain
Aries, Leos, Virgo sun signs do ensure personal goals are tempered with restraint

In personal life control means to act to get good outcomes and avoid bad ones
Auditors examine the control environments; we need to consult doctors at once
These independent outsiders are a third eye to examine if controls are in balance
For lack of controls, companies go into bankruptcy and people become delinquent

The best-managed companies encounter recessions and end-of-life-cycle pangs
Focus on being grateful and stop developing prejudice and discrimination fangs
Our bodies and minds are subject to attrition and disease, a spoiler of our plans
Accept changed situations, smile and pray if you encounter irregular CAT scans

Tidy Investments

Personal fortune or financial net worth is treated as an index of personal success
Living paycheck to paycheck means millions are creatures who are dispossessed
Your holdings of cash, real estate, insurances and automobiles a planner will assess
A financial cushion needs you to save for a rainy day, so avoid enjoying in excess

Money does buy conveniences, seldom happiness – invest in a good education
That will help you graduate with a chance of better career earnings and choices
You can then hold your head high, the increased self-esteem will help you rejoice
When returns are erratic, try recalling the president who was a senator of Illinois

An investment in happy and stable family ties brings rich and varied dividends
Fairweather friends provide at times comfort, but only in family ties can one depend
Children raised in a loving family show discipline and values they learn frontend
Learning to eat simple and varied meals and showing respect starts a cultured trend

Returns on investment must be analyzed for both financial and non-financial goals
Net-worth measures your finances, checking life's net worth is a safer poll of polls
It measures the metrics of your positive habits, traits, emotions – all useful controls
Your knowledge, skills and good health provides a safe ride through life's potholes

Bucket List

Turning 60 is a personal milestone, exciting thoughts fill the mind's recesses
Plans and revisions are like writing a will then a codicil, looks very impressive
Threescore years of infirmities slow life like a river delta, you get defensive
The receding hairline and swollen tummy dampen the mood that is festive

Plan to slow my cognitive decline, build my immunity, stave off dementia
Warn my family of developing Parkinson's, stop spices to avoid dyspepsia
Play sudoku and solve crosswords to steady the brain, an organ so precious
I have now a master blueprint, my wife cautions it looks very pretentious

A holistic plan should consider my personal trinity; body, mind and soul
My belief in God is steady; asked him to open doors, he opened windows
With constant prayer I persevere, I understand the unbeliever's innuendo
They find answers in life using reason, God's door will always remain open

I did honest labour for 40 years, it helped pay for groceries and pare down debt
Luckily my wife was a simple Jane, she never seemed to require a Corvette
Or cruises or investment portfolios; we hear songs on our favourite cassette
My bucket list has no smart plans, we plan to ride on life's pious driftnet

Long Road

Our forebears moved to cities some centuries ago, taking the untrodden road
From raw feudalism to ripe capitalism, a new beginning did this thought bode
This new utopia would usher us freedom, perfect competition and emancipation
Few benefits did the common folk see, what alone increased were their privations

The wise then reckoned that communism would make to our lives a quantum leap
And promised us a new millennium, and we would emerge from our beauty sleep
In a Godless world, we will share nature's store and will our lives make whole
We ended up as serfs to a godless state, and that nearly made us lose our souls

A tested road we can take and seek the hand of God, by asking him to walk in tow
He has no economic creed, just asks us to on our neighbours our wealth bestow
We must not accumulate; it will cause our bodies harm and make us hoarders be
The book of life teaches us that our loving God knows all our adversities

This planet we can set aglow by practising empathy to our friends next door
To nature restore its primeval beauty and thus our creator adore
In helping our neighbours, we restore humanity and this earth a paradise make
If we our brother's keeper be, this simple wisdom will have no need to recalibrate

Scandal

The wise men said in days bygone 'if you sit while I stand, you won't see what I see'
And if you climb a coconut tree while I stand down, you will still not see what I see
Oh, Canada, as sons we stand on guard for thee and wish to be glorious and free
Teach us how to be a good trustee, and for posterity treat our sons with dignity

Let's not compel our doctor sons to drive cabbies but guardians of our health be
Realize managing human resources is not hiring and firing but enhancing ability
And don't let our sons and daughters take up positions of extreme mediocrity
To maintain their dignity, use their skills and expertise, it makes good fiscal policy

The company balance sheet that tells us of its net worth omits its pivotal asset
How myopic they can be omitting the most precious resource – that's you and me
We are a land of only 37 million, full employment should our goal be
Putting everyone to work in skills they command, not in funk hole content be

Such simple sanity; we as citizens must from our politicians demand accountability
Not permitting to sway us with their inanities like balancing books or austerity
The pillars of our economy must be both you and me and food for our families
True patriot love will then in our sons be and will kinder in us a notable alchemy

Cultural Threads

Indian, Chinese and Egyptian culture each have treads that form a rich tapestry
The Indian namaste means I bow to you; it's disarming, making you feel like family
Colourful festivals like Holi and Diwali celebrate the harvest and invoke prosperity
Joint families soon disappearing once welded kindred even in times of adversity

The love with temples is scientific, being built on the earth's magnetic wave lines
The copper plate below the idol radiates positive energy to those in its confines
The arranged marriage is an odious concept but is more durable than dating lines
Marriage is a sacrament; no easy divorce, lessening fear of marriage landmines

In Egypt love blooms, they are so friendly and loving, go see them in Khan Khalili
The Cairo Bridge is filled with lovers whose overtures display healthy spontaneity
The food is phenomenal, humor astounding, tourists love ancient Egyptian deities
Don't miss the famed Nile cruise and the belly dance, save a photo for posterity

Confucius virtues are the hallmark of Chinese etiquette, kindness and honesty
Home is their pivot; try succulent Peking duck and hotpot, avoid talk of ideology
A strong work ethic, paying homage to their ancestors and serving their motherland
These cultural threads weave a story for all to learn; wear a harmony armband

CPSIA information can be obtained
at www.ICGtesting.com
Printed in the USA
BVHW020315081021
618472BV00002B/6

9 781039 114326